BUSINESS BUILDERS

IN REAL ESTATE

JACK DOUGLAS came to Sun City to interview Del Webb and feature the town in his "America" television series.

Sun City Most Famous Town Of Its Kind In United States

How famous is Sun City? *The most famous (retirement community) (planned community) (resort-retirement community) in America! Take your pick.*

How can we make this statement? Easy!

Name any other such town featured by virtually every major magazine in America, network television, thousands of newspapers and even made a "household word" for

Sun City Like Camelot, It Has Something 'Special'

In his stageplay Alan Lerner wrote: "In Camelot it never rains till after sundown." Sun Citians think their town is something special, too.

The Del E. Webb Development Co. has provided the community facilities — admittedly above the ordinary — but it's the people who *really* make Sun City bloom.

Del Webb himself forecast this when Sun City opened in 1960. He said:

"*Concrete, steel and lumber can make the buildings, but people make the community. Together we can realize a way-of-life unprecedented in America.*"

The kind of people who move to Sun City are special in the pioneering spirit they possess — in their desire to do something with retirement except idle it away in a rocking chair.

We think you'll find this birthday issue proof that Mr. Webb's prediction, "People make the community," is true of Sun City, Ariz.

* * * *

retirement by such comedians as Bob Hope, Rowan and Martin, Carol Burnett and Steve Allen?

National exposure started with a bang when dozens of travel writers on a swing through the West toured and reported on Sun City several weeks after it opened.

(Continued on Page 4)

ROBERT PRESTON cooled off in a Sun City pool as he starred in an hour-long color "special" on ABC-TV. **BELOW** — Encyclopaedia Brittanica filmed Sun City activities, including Rhythm Ramblers, for its movie division.

LIFE MAGAZINE spent a day photographing Sun City, setting up scenes like this chaise lounge brigade. **BELOW** — National Geographic, among dozens of magazines which have reported on Sun City, was attracted by a cactus landscape.

Demonstrating that shrewd real-estate deals can not only be profitable but can also transform the way people live, Del Webb developed the first community—Sun City—built and marketed specifically for senior citizens. This advertisement shows several of Sun City's features, including a pool and a community band.

BUSINESS BUILDERS IN REAL ESTATE

Nathan Aaseng

The Oliver Press, Inc.
Minneapolis

Heritage Middle School IMC
121 W. Butler Avenue
West St. Paul, MN 55118

The Oliver Press, Inc.
Charlotte Square
5707 West 36th Street
Minneapolis, MN 55416-2510

Library of Congress Cataloging-in-Publication Data
Aaseng, Nathan.
Business Builders in Real Estate/Nathan Aaseng.
p. cm. — (Business builders)
Includes bibliographical references and index.
    Summary: Profiles seven real estate developers, including John Nicholson, John Jacob Astor,
William Levitt, Del Webb, Walt Disney, Paul Reichmann, and the Ghermezian brothers.
ISBN 1-881508-79-X
1. Real estate developers—United States—Biography—Juvenile literature. 2. Real estate busi-
ness—United States—Biography—Juvenile literature. 3. Businesspeople—United States—
Biography—Juvenile literature. [1. Real estate developers. 2. Businesspeople.] I. Title. II.
Series.

HD255 .A57 2002
333.73'15'092273—dc21
[B]

                                                          2001036369
                                                             CIP
                                                              AC

ISBN 1-881508-79-X
Printed in the United States of America

08 07 06 05 04 03 02   8 7 6 5 4 3 2 1

CONTENTS

INTRODUCTION
RICHES AND RUIN

In 1966, Mel Powers scraped together $2,000 for a down payment to buy an old, empty, rundown building in Houston, Texas, that nobody else wanted. He fixed it up and set out to attract tenants for the building. His timing was good. Many of Houston's largest businesses were tied to the oil industry, and soaring oil profits during the 1960s triggered a boom in the city's economy. This—along with the transfer of the massive National Aeronautics and Space Administration (NASA) headquarters to Houston beginning in 1962—created a far greater demand for both housing and office space than was available in the city. Once Powers's building was attractively refurbished, he had no trouble filling it with paying tenants.

down payment: money paid immediately for a purchase, with the remainder to be paid later

In areas with highly coveted real estate—such as New York City, shown here in 1936—land and the developments on it change hands at extremely high prices. These high-stakes deals can bring fortune or ruin to those in the real-estate business.

invest: to commit money to some enterprise, usually a business, in order to get more money or some other value in return

tenant: someone who rents property, such as office space or an apartment, from the owner of a building

bankrupt: having been legally determined as unable to pay back one's debts. A court then divides up the debtor's property among the creditors.

The scarcity of building space in the city boosted rents and made Powers's property appealing to investors. Less than a year after Powers acquired the building, he sold it for $110,000. Having seen the substantial profit that could be made by improving properties, Powers threw himself wholeheartedly into the real-estate development business. For more than a decade, he bought one plot of land after another, constructed or refurbished buildings on the properties, filled them with tenants, and then sold them to real-estate investors at a great profit. By 1979, he had constructed buildings worth more than $200 million.

Powers channeled some of his earnings into a far-flung business empire. As the money rolled in, he settled into a life of comfort and prestige. He purchased helicopters for himself and custom-ordered a $3 million yacht equipped with such luxuries as gold-plated sinks. With what seemed a guaranteed formula for making money, his extravagant lifestyle appeared to pose no problem.

In the early 1980s, however, oil prices nosedived. Houston's economy came to a screeching halt. Some businesses went bankrupt; many others had to lay off employees and reduce office expenses. Believing he was financially strong enough to weather the business slump, Powers continued his strategy of buying urban land and constructing large office buildings.

But the economic tailspin continued until, by 1983, almost one-third of all the office space in Houston was empty. With such slack demand, the prices that owners could charge tenants dropped.

Powers, who had spent heavily on new construction, now found himself stuck with empty buildings and declining rental income. The value of his properties plummeted. Buckling under huge debts and no income, 46-year-old Powers had to sell off all of his properties for whatever they would bring. In the course of little more than a year, Powers lost everything. He went from a fabulously wealthy real-estate baron to bankruptcy and disappeared from public life completely.

Such is the wild roller coaster ride of the real-estate business.

SELLING THE EARTH

The real-estate business, the buying and selling of land and whatever is on that land, is a relatively new enterprise in North America. The practice did not exist among the Native American tribes that inhabited the continent for thousands of years. These people thought of land as a communal resource. For many Native American groups, their bond with the land held religious significance. They considered the earth to be a powerful presence that gave them life and sustenance. The idea of sectioning off the earth into plots to be bought and sold was as shocking to them as the idea of selling the wind, or the warmth of the sun, or their own mothers.

Therefore, while different tribes often claimed the exclusive right to live and hunt in a given territory, they did not recognize the right of individuals to own sections of that land. Although many agricultural tribes established permanent dwellings that were their property, they did not equate these with real estate. Even the sturdiest of houses was only temporary, like clothes upon a body, while the earth was everlasting.

Beginning with Christopher Columbus in 1492, European explorers and settlers brought to North America the European tradition of law that treated land as a commodity. Like clothing, manufactured goods, and works of art, land was something that people could own as a personal possession. It, along with all improvements made upon it, could be bought and sold.

Countless treaties and land purchases were made between the settlers and the Native Americans, both of whom had distinctly different views of the nature of land ownership. This clash of cultures over the idea of ownership of land led to confusion and conflict. Eventually, the Europeans were able to impose their system of land acquisition on the continent's original inhabitants. They used their familiarity with the intricacies of this system to push the Indians off of their traditional lands and onto ever-dwindling reservations.

RIGHT OF DISCOVERY

From the Europeans' perspective, the discovery of North America was the greatest real-estate windfall in the history of the world. Dismissing the occupants of the continent as ignorant savages, they viewed the lands as being basically without owners. Almost overnight, millions upon millions of acres of land were suddenly available for the taking.

Under European laws of discovery, however, individuals could not simply sail over and grab whatever they found. The first adventurers to arrive in a region they thought was uncivilized claimed the area for their country, which then set the policy for selling or distributing that land to individuals or organizations.

LAND SPECULATION

Many early U.S. citizens, including some of the most prominent, became intrigued with the risky business of real estate. Investment in land was particularly attractive because it was one of the few ways that a person of modest means in the colonial United States could hope to make a fortune. Those who found themselves locked in the grip of debt were

William Penn (1644-1718) was one of the greatest beneficiaries of the European system of distributing land. Penn obtained the title to millions of acres of wilderness from the king of England as payment of a debt to his family. Penn (center, standing with arms outstretched) established the colony of Pennsylvania on the land, maintaining friendly relations with the Indians who lived there.

especially inclined to take a chance on real estate as a last hope for avoiding debtor's prison.

The reason that real estate was, and continues to be, such an unpredictable tightrope walk between riches and ruin is because the product that is bought and sold can change so drastically over time. A piece of land that today lies in a worthless, mosquito-infested swamp may, over the course of time, become a coveted piece of suburban property. Crime and neglect may turn a fashionable downtown business district into a rundown, unsafe neighborhood where no one wants to shop. The discovery of oil on a property has been known to increase its value more than 1,000 times almost overnight. A single event,

such as the building of a freeway, can increase property values of businesses that depend upon access to good transportation, while decreasing the values of homes whose once-quiet neighborhood suddenly borders a noisy highway.

When real-estate investors think about buying a piece of property, they give more consideration to what the property might become than to what it is. Heavy investment in land or any other commodity in the hope that its value will rise considerably is known as speculation. Since predicting the future is an uncertain enterprise at best, mistakes in speculating are as common as savvy investments.

Normally, real estate gains value over time. The amount of land in a country is fixed, and, as the population grows, the amount of available land becomes more scarce and more precious. But the real-estate market also rises and falls according to local economic conditions. Few investors can afford to sit and wait out extended periods of low market value. This is because real estate is so expensive that even the wealthiest buyers generally take out loans to make their purchases. They count on their real estate appreciating in value to offset the cost of paying interest on the loans and of paying high property taxes. If the real estate does not gain in value or produce high rent revenues, owners may be unable to meet their payments. Banks can then foreclose, or assume ownership of the property. In that case, the real-estate investor loses his or her entire investment.

Some early American land speculators, such as George Washington, made out well in their buying

rent revenues: money brought in to an owner of properties from rent paid by tenants

George Washington (1732-1799), who would become the first president of the United States, bought more than 7,000 acres of land for his Mount Vernon plantation.

recession: a period of general decline in business activity

and selling of land. Many others, including Vice President Aaron Burr and Revolutionary War hero Harry Lee (the father of Civil War general Robert E. Lee), were ruined by it.

GAMBLING

In many ways, the real-estate business today is not much different than it was during the lifetimes of Washington, Burr, and Lee. It remains a business that can create fabulous wealth for a shrewd investor. With so many risks involved and only so much land to go around, the potential earnings in real estate are astronomical. Experts estimate that in the United States, twice as much money changes hands in real estate as it does in all other businesses combined.

Real estate is as much of a gamble as it ever was. Although an understanding of business principles is crucial in navigating the turbulent waters of the real-estate world, success still depends, to some extent, upon an ability to predict the future. A person can use all the research data in the world to gauge the amount of income per square foot of office space needed to make a potential deal profitable, only to have the figures rendered meaningless by a sudden recession.

For many of the biggest operators in the real-estate world, it is precisely this element of risk—and the dependence on their own predictions and business skills to guide them safely through it—that appeals to them. The thrill that some people get from risking a quarter in a slot machine in the hope of winning a few hundred dollars is magnified many times over when a real-estate developer places a billion-dollar bet on a piece of property. Billionaire Canadian developer Paul Reichmann admitted to friends, "My religion won't let me go to Las Vegas. *This* is my Las Vegas."

BIG DEALS

Speculators such as Burr and Lee were willing to risk their entire savings on land schemes in the hope of making their families financially secure for life. But for many real-estate tycoons today, the business has become more of a game than a means of making a living. The most successful real-estate moguls generally have far more money than they could possibly hope to spend in several lifetimes. Yet they remain among the most active players in the field. It is commonly said in the real-estate business that for the high rollers, "money is just a way of keeping score."

tycoon: a rich businessperson or industrialist

mogul: someone who is very rich or powerful

Donald Trump is perhaps the most famous modern example of a real-estate wheeler and dealer who stays active in the business not so much for the money, but because he loves what he does. The son of a contractor who built low- and middle-income housing, Trump had followed his dad around construction sites almost from the time he could walk. His experience with the building world and his flair for drama led him to move into a bold venture while he was still in college. Going through a list of properties whose owners were unable to make their loan payments, he discovered an apartment complex in Cincinnati. The place had fallen on such hard times that 800 of its 1,200 units stood empty.

contractor: someone who agrees to provide services and/or material, usually for construction work, for a certain price

"I do it [real-estate deals] to do it," Donald Trump (b. 1946) once said. "That's how I get my kicks."

Taking the real-estate developer's view that the value of a property is not its present worth but its future worth, Trump took a chance. Using borrowed money, he obtained the undesirable building for half of what it would have cost him to build it and invested $800,000 in renovations. Once the place looked appealing, he was able to attract tenants and charge higher rents. By the time he sold it a few years later, the complex was worth $6 million more than he had paid for it.

This set Trump on a career of high-stakes real-estate projects, including the 68-story Trump Tower, which earned him an incredible fortune. Even when he had more money than he could count, however, Trump lived for real-estate transactions. "Deals are my art form," Trump wrote in an autobiography.

"Other people paint beautifully on canvas or write wonderful poetry. I like making deals, preferably big deals."

This book tells the stories of some of the biggest real-estate deals ever made and the people who made them. Most of these people realized incredible profits; some were spectacular failures. All of them changed the face of the communities in which they bought and developed. A few dreamed up and carried out real-estate deals so daring that they actually altered the way people lived.

The Trump Tower is the tallest residential building in New York City.

1

JOHN NICHOLSON

BETTING ON THE NEW NATION

No one disputed that John Nicholson was a financial genius. One Pennsylvania official, astounded at how Nicholson was able to untangle government finances following the American Revolution, told him, "I wish I had you [for] only one day." Nicholson used that financial expertise to gain control over an astounding four million acres of Pennsylvania land.

Not only was Nicholson gifted in financial matters, but his record as a public official also seemed solid. Nicholson refused to take bribes. Even when he desperately needed the money, he turned down on principle a chance to make a huge profit by engaging in the slave trade. Nicholson was a compassionate man who did much to aid the cause of military veterans and war widows. He maintained an

finances: money, usually of a government or corporation

Believing in the potential for growth and prosperity in the United States, John Nicholson (1757?-1800) supported the development of a federal city.

unshakable belief that the United States was destined to become one of the great nations of the world, and he worked hard to help make it happen. Largely through his efforts, Washington, D.C., was transformed from a hot, mosquito-infested wilderness into a thriving city.

Still, Nicholson was willing to be dishonest in order to get the land he wanted, and he used his government position and contacts to gain favors to buy land. To top it off, he managed to entangle himself in one of the greatest real-estate fiascoes of all time. His struggles to escape his plight only made matters worse. In the end, his staggering debts landed him in debtor's prison and brought friends, partners, and shareholders to ruin.

A TALENT FOR GOVERNMENT FINANCES

Little is known about Nicholson's early life, other than that he was born in Wales in about 1757 and came to the American colonies with his family sometime before the American Revolution. The family settled in Pennsylvania and lived there long enough for John to become solidly American in his sympathies. When the War of Independence broke out, he joined the First Pennsylvania Regiment of the Continental Army and earned the rank of sergeant. Nicholson's superiors recognized his gift for organizing finances, and, in October 1778, they appointed him to the position of clerk in the Board of Treasury of the Continental Congress. One of his primary responsibilities as clerk was to verify pay claims of government officers.

pay claim: a form submitted to a government or company that requests money owed for services or labor already performed

On March 8, 1781, Nicholson resigned his post to accept a job as auditor, or examiner, of accounts for the state of Pennsylvania. About a year later, on April 28, he married Hannah Duncan, but he was so consumed by his overwhelming duties that his family life suffered. Frustrated by the lack of attention, Hannah often left home and took the children with her. Although John begged her to come back, she stayed with her parents or her sister in New York for many months at a time.

Meanwhile, Nicholson performed his government duties so well that he was named Pennsylvania's comptroller-general, the man in charge of the state's finances. Like many states, Pennsylvania came out of the war owing a great deal of money to the soldiers

The Second Continental Congress declared America's independence from Great Britain in 1776. The Congress would later employ Nicholson as a clerk.

John Nicholson's wife, Hannah Duncan, and the couple's second child, John Nicholson Jr. The couple would have eight children altogether.

While serving as the disposer of Loyalist estates, Nicholson had 900 lawsuits brought against him, all charging him with diverting parts of the estates for his own use.

who fought on its behalf. In addition, the federal government asked the states to help pay off the debt it had built up operating the Continental Army and Continental Congress. Short of massive taxation, the only way for Pennsylvania to pay off the debts was in the form of land. The state had 22 million acres available to give army veterans as payment for services, and Nicholson had the responsibility of overseeing the distribution program. He was also assigned to dispose of the estates of Loyalists who had supported the British during the war and had since fled the country.

The task of supervising the payment of debts through the distribution of land was a massive job, but Nicholson performed it quickly. Under his direction, Pennsylvania managed to pay off its war debts faster than any of its neighboring states. In 12 years as comptroller-general, Nicholson cleared up 24,000 outstanding accounts.

THE LURE OF REAL ESTATE

It was in the course of this land distribution that Nicholson first became attracted to real estate as an investment. He noted that Pennsylvania's population was growing rapidly, from 360,000 in 1787 to nearly 435,000 in 1791. This caused an increase in the demand for land, which boosted the land's value. Nicholson's position gave him an enormous advantage in entering the field of real estate. He had access to all of the surveying documents and knew where the best land parcels were located and who would receive them.

surveying documents: papers outlining the results of surveying, or the measuring of the distances and the elevations of a piece of land

Many of the veterans were so cash-strapped that they were eager to sell the land they received in payment. Nicholson saw this as a good money-making opportunity, which was especially appealing because his job as comptroller-general paid poorly. Realizing that some would consider it improper for a man in charge of land distribution to get involved in land sales, he got a friend to handle the transactions, using fictitious names for the buyers.

Then, in 1787, Pennsylvania assumed its share of the federal debt by issuing new loan certificates. Anyone who held loan certificates from the federal government could exchange those for the new state certificates. These certificates could then be converted to titles to state lands. Nicholson bought so

impeachment: the charging of a public official with improper conduct in office

many of these new loan certificates that he was charged with using his office to obtain them illegally. This eventually led to impeachment charges against him in 1793, of which Nicholson was narrowly acquitted.

INGENIOUS STRATEGY

More land became available in the early 1790s, when Pennsylvania acquired land from the Iroquois Indians in the northwest part of the state. Nicholson, who was becoming more and more fascinated by the possibilities of real estate, played a major role in obtaining these lands.

By this time, Nicholson had developed an ingenious strategy for making a fortune off the land. He bought large tracts of land, then attracted settlers by offering some of it to them at a low price. As long as the land was unoccupied wilderness, it would not appreciate much in value. Since Nicholson borrowed money for most of his purchases and paid high interest rates on the loans, he risked great financial loss if his land didn't appreciate in value. But as soon as the settlers began building up prosperous communities, the land would become attractive to businesses and other settlers. In that case, the value of the land would increase.

appreciate: to rise in value, especially over time

"Every settler in a New Country gives a value to all the circumjacent land," Nicholson wrote. "A person who owns only a Single Tract, when he improves it or causes it to be improved, is indirectly giving half of his labor to others." Nicholson decided to take advantage of this "free" labor. He reasoned that all he had to do was hold on to the land border-ing on the settlers' land and wait for them to do the work of improving it.

GAINING INFLUENCE

Meanwhile, the Pennsylvania government lost con-trol of its plans for the orderly sale and distribution of the land. Through corruption and incompetence, the surveying crews produced inaccurate reports. Records were so poorly kept that the state land office was not sure which lands had been sold or which were currently occupied. Some parcels of land were sold to several different buyers at the same time.

While Nicholson was scrupulous about rejecting bribes, he was not above behind-the-scenes maneu-vering to work the system in his favor. He went out of his way to cultivate friendships with other officials who might prove to be useful contacts in financial dealings. Nicholson was such an opportunist in this regard that he frequently switched political parties, depending on which he thought was advocating poli-cies most useful to him.

Among the friends he made were influential peo-ple in the land office. They could tell him when demand for land was high and when it ebbed, as well as identify who was competing against him in his bids for land. Whenever a dispute arose over the ownership of any of his lands, Nicholson could count on his friends to rule in his favor. If need be, he would have them backdate the documents so that he would appear to have been the first purchaser of the land, even if that were not the case.

At one point, Nicholson urged rejection of the pro-posed U.S. Constitution because he was afraid it might restrict his powers as a state official.

Nicholson had many people working for him to find the best land. Daniel Brodhead was an especially important contact who gave Nicholson inside information in exchange for money or land. Brodhead also backdated documents for Nicholson.

Nicholson also made important contacts among surveyors. These people knew which lands were valuable and which were not. They could hide the true value of the land from settlers, who would then be willing to sell for less than the land was worth.

In addition to using the aid of his land office friends to make favorable deals, Nicholson took advantage of others' financial difficulties. For example, James Wilson, a signer of the Declaration of Independence and one of the authors of the U.S. Constitution, got himself into major trouble in land speculation. He had purchased over a million acres of land west of the Allegheny Mountains, hoping to reap a large profit when it appreciated in value. In

speculation: investment in land or any other commodity in the hope of a quick, large profit

James Wilson (1742-1798), a Pennsylvania delegate to the Constitutional Convention of 1787, would eventually go to debtor's prison because of the state of his finances.

the process, however, he plunged so deeply into debt that he could not meet his loan payments. He was in danger of losing both his lands and his personal fortune.

About 200,000 acres of Wilson's land conflicted with claims made by Nicholson. Wilson was so desperate for cash to pay debts that he could not afford a legal battle. He had to settle the dispute by selling his claims to Nicholson for a fraction of what the deal was worth.

BUYING SPREE

Nicholson became obsessed with buying as much land as he could, always taking pains to hide his involvement from the public. In 1792, he gained title to most of a large area of land known as the Erie Triangle, which he had helped Pennsylvania purchase from the Iroquois Indians.

That same year, the country experienced a severe economic depression. Prices of products and the value of land fell so drastically that many people's fortunes evaporated. Nicholson not only survived this tough time but actually gained more land from it. Desperate land speculators were willing to give up their lands for whatever they could get for them. Nicholson pocketed a great number of these cheap properties.

In the course of a few years, Nicholson became the major landowner in Pennsylvania. Yet because he used agents and fictitious names and operated through land companies of which he was the major shareholder, he managed to hide the extent of his

Conflicting land claims in Pennsylvania were settled by the Board of Property. John Nicholson knew all of the men on the Board of Property.

depression: a period of drastic decline in business production and of high unemployment

shareholder: someone who owns a portion of a company, in the form of shares of stock

purchases. Nicholson borrowed large amounts of money to make all of these deals. By 1794, he was deeply in debt to three different banks, none of which knew of his other debts.

Nicholson came up with what seemed like a brilliant plan for increasing the value of his property. He offered to give 150 acres to the first 50 families who agreed to settle on certain sections of land that he owned. The next 100 would get 100 free acres. Meanwhile, he lobbied hard to get the state government to build roads and other improvements to make the settlements accessible and attractive. He did whatever he could to develop the wilderness into thriving communities that would increase the value of the land. In order to guarantee a ready supply of food for the settlers, he became one of the largest flour distributors in the area.

PROBLEMS

But Nicholson's plan ran into an unforeseen problem. Many of the Iroquois were angry about the sale of their land. Spurred on by British agents who were determined to make trouble for Americans along the Canadian frontier, the Iroquois engaged in skirmishes with pioneer settlers. This, along with economic factors, discouraged Pennsylvanians from undertaking the backbreaking work of trying to carve a new community out of the wilderness. By 1795, only four families had settled in all of what is now Erie County. Nicholson never came close to attracting enough settlers to bring about the increase in land value that he had expected.

Nevertheless, Nicholson refused to give up on his investments. When one land company failed, he bought out his discouraged partners and organized another. Eventually, he consolidated all of his land companies into a giant corporation—the North American Land Company. At one time, it controlled more than six million acres of land. Nicholson used some of this land, on which he owed a sizable debt, as collateral, or a guarantee, for more loans. The increasingly complex web of financial deals that he wove to stave off creditors and salvage his dream took so much time and effort that he retired from government to devote all his energy to it.

collateral: property offered against a loan in case the debtor cannot pay it back

creditor: a person or company that has loaned money not yet paid back

SEARCHING FOR A MIRACLE

As his financial problems continued to mount, Nicholson looked for a miracle to solve them. But everything he tried only dug him more deeply into debt. He and his land company partners arranged to purchase two million acres of land in Georgia. But Nicholson did not take the time to inspect the property before buying it. The land turned out to be worth far less than he had been promised. Some of his partners suddenly informed him that they were broke and could not meet their financial obligations in the deal. Lacking any cash of his own, Nicholson could not pay the taxes, and much of his land was confiscated.

Nicholson then tried to set up a special community, which he named Asylum, for the many French aristocrats who had fled to the United States to escape the bloody French Revolution. He went so far as to construct nearly 50 houses in advance, along with shops and businesses that would provide the French settlers with everything they would need. Unfortunately, most of the refugees were not interested in becoming permanent residents of the United States; they were just biding their time until they could return to France. The plan succeeded only in creating one of the first ghost towns in the country.

Nicholson's most ambitious scheme involved the new nation's capital of Washington, D.C. George Washington had hoped to finance the building of the capital by auctioning off lots on which people could build homes and businesses. But that had failed. Few people were willing to take a chance on paying good money for plots in this unappealing

An advertisement outlining the terms for buying lots in the new federal city, Washington, D.C.

TERMS of SALE of LOTS in the CITY of WASH-INGTON, the Eighth Day of *October*, 1792.

ALL Lands purchafed at this Sale, are to be fubject to the Terms and Conditions declared by the Prefident, purfuant to the Deeds in Truft.

The purchafer is immediately to pay one fourth part of the purchafe money; the refidue is to be paid in three equal annual payments, with yearly intereft of fix per cent. on the whole principal unpaid: If any payment is not made at the day, the payments made are to be forfeited, or the whole principal and intereft unpaid may be recovered on one fuit and execution, in the option of the Commiffioners.

The purchafer is to be entitled to a conveyance, on the whole purchafe money and intereft being paid, and not before. No bid under Three Dollars to be received.

wilderness with the stifling climate. There were widespread doubts that the city would ever be built.

Nicholson, however, believed the federal city was going to be everything George Washington had envisioned and more. Buying land there would be a once-in-a-lifetime economic opportunity. "All other places have risen by slow degrees," he declared. "This will astonish the world by its rapidity; the people are all ready and only wait for houses to rush in."

In partnership with Senator Robert Morris, whom he had known from his years in Pennsylvania government, and James Greenleaf, a 28-year-old Bostonian merchant who offered financial support, Nicholson hatched a plan to monopolize building lots in the proposed new city. The three arranged to buy 6,000 lots from the government with the promise that they would develop a certain percentage of the property within a timeline set by the government. In addition, they purchased 1,200 lots from private owners.

When it turned out that Greenleaf didn't have the credit line he had claimed to have, Nicholson scrambled frantically to find loans to finance the partners' project. Greenleaf offered to buy his partners' shares of the failing project, but Nicholson, convinced that the land in Washington was valuable, persuaded Morris to help him buy out Greenleaf's share instead. This increased Nicholson's staggering debt load.

Nicholson and Morris spent $120,000 on construction on their properties. Not only did they build houses, but they also brought a great deal of

James Greenleaf sold John Nicholson and Robert Morris on the idea of investing in the new federal city. He claimed that he had a $1 million line of credit in the Netherlands that he would contribute to the partnership, but this turned out to be false—Dutch banks refused to do business with Greenleaf.

The Seven Buildings, stretching from 1901 to 1913 Pennsylvania Avenue in Washington, D.C., were built by Nicholson and Morris. The corner building served as a temporary State Department from 1800 to 1801, and it is shown here being used as military head-quarters during the Civil War.

industry to the new capital. They constructed some of the first stores and bakeries in Washington, D.C., as well as lumberyards, ironworks, canals, and the largest hotel in the city. Nicholson spent a great deal of time between 1795 and 1797 organizing the effort—getting supplies for his contractors and finding money to pay the workers. He was so heavily involved, in fact, that Morris warned him, "I think you are too often employed in doing what ought to be done by others; correct this error and you will accomplish more real business in a short time than any other man living."

Despite Nicholson's efforts, the Washington project fared no better than any of his other money-making schemes. The federal district commissioners concentrated their construction in the one area of the proposed town where Nicholson and Morris had not bought lots. Despite their persistent sales efforts, the two managed to sell only 1,000 of their 7,200 lots in 18 months.

By 1798, Nicholson was spiraling toward disaster. He owed money to many individuals—bankers, government officials, architects, workers, agents; the list seemed endless. Meanwhile, friends to whom he had lent money over the years sheepishly told him they had no money to repay him.

For a brief time, he and Morris kept afloat by endorsing each other's bank notes. Bankers who dealt with Nicholson assumed he would pay them back because the respected Morris vouched for him,

This building on 9th and Pennsylvania Avenues in Washington, D.C., was built in 1795 for John Nicholson. Originally a hotel, it later became a tavern managed by William Tunnicliff, who changed the name to Tunnicliff's Tavern.

Although Robert Morris (1734-1806) has become known as the financier of the American Revolution, some historians now think that while controlling the finances of the war, he may have taken $80,000 out of money meant for the revolutionary cause. Morris would eventually go to debtor's prison for more than three years because of his unpaid debts.

When they arrived in debtor's prison, Robert Morris and John Nicholson found that their ex-partner, James Greenleaf, was already there.

while those who dealt with Morris assumed he was trustworthy because of Nicholson's endorsement. Soon, however, neither man had a reputation that banks would trust. Unable to get money to pay taxes, Nicholson lost much of his land. He could not sell many of his properties—even at cut-rate prices—because he had used them so many times as collateral that no one was sure who held the titles anymore. When it became apparent that Nicholson owed far more money than he could ever hope to repay, he spent much of 1798 running and hiding from creditors and sheriffs.

In 1799, the authorities caught up with Nicholson in Philadelphia and placed him in debtor's prison. Exhausted, he died there on December 5, 1800, at the age of 43, leaving behind an incredible debt of some $12 million.

LEGACY

Although John Nicholson made a horrific mess of his finances, his real-estate dealings played an important role in the early growth of the United States. His schemes to develop his vast land holdings resulted in many road and water transportation improvements, most notably the Lancaster Turnpike in Pennsylvania. Nicholson laid the groundwork for the eventual settlement of western Pennsylvania by promoting settlement and establishing such necessities as ironworks and a dependable flour trade.

At a time when virtually every other investor shied away from the federal government's ambitious plans to build a capital city in the middle of nowhere,

Nicholson plunged in with energy and optimism. He took the initiative in building houses and bringing manufacturing equipment and expertise into the federal district. According to author Robert Arbuckle, "that the city existed at all in the 1790s was due very largely to the efforts of Nicholson and his partners." Nicholson's tireless promotional efforts eventually did inspire others to finally take a chance and invest in Washington, D.C., although this success came too late to save him from financial ruin. Thanks largely to Nicholson and his partners, the federal government moved into the new capital on schedule in 1800.

Nicholson's heirs were plagued by creditors suing them for more than 40 years after his death.

One of Nicholson's land improvements, the Lancaster Turnpike, stretched across 62 miles and was called the best highway of its day. Part of the route is shown here in 1942 near Paradise, Pennsylvania.

2

JOHN JACOB ASTOR

MANHATTAN: THE ISLAND OF GOLD

In 1810, John Jacob Astor sold a lot near Wall Street on Manhattan Island, New York, for $8,000. Once the contract was signed, the buyer expressed his glee over the deal he had negotiated. Smugly, he told Astor that he intended to resell the lot in a few years for $12,000.

Astor conceded that the buyer was probably right. But then he went on to say what he intended to do with the $8,000 from the sale. "I shall buy 80 lots above Canal Street, and by the time your one lot is worth $12,000, my 80 lots will be worth $80,000."

It was a bold boast for rural lands that were presently worth only a very small fraction of that amount. Few of his contemporaries believed that the city of New York would expand within their lifetimes

John Jacob Astor (1763-1848) built successful businesses in the musical instrument trade, in the fur trade, and in real estate. His investments in Manhattan real estate would make him New York's first millionaire, with one of the most envied fortunes in history.

A 1938 view of Wall Street, now New York's famous financial district, where Astor sold his lot for $8,000

to cover the area Astor was talking about. But when it came to glowing over the future growth of the United States, John Jacob Astor was a kindred spirit to John Nicholson. Astor knew the island of Manhattan would be a gold mine. With its fine natural harbor leading into one of the most established cities on the eastern coast of the United States, he believed it had the potential to become one of the world's foremost business centers.

Astor's foresight was rewarded. New York grew more quickly than any city in the nation, turning Manhattan into the most expensive real estate in the world. Astor, who owned a large chunk of the island, cashed in on the growth and became the wealthiest man in the United States.

THE BUTCHER'S UNHAPPY SON

John Jacob Astor was born on July 17, 1763, in Waldorf, a small village near Heidelberg, Germany. His father, a butcher, had a reputation for being a lazy, quarrelsome drunkard. Although he was able to provide a decent living for his family during harvest time, they went hungry for much of the year. As soon as they were old enough, Jacob's older brothers left home to seek their fortunes. Jacob's mother died when he was about 14 years old, and he was left with his father and a stepmother who did not like him.

Jacob was an exceptional student. One of his teachers remarked that he had "a clear head, and everything right behind the ears." But the family had no money to pay for his training in any profession, so he submitted to a dreary life of learning the butcher's trade from his father. He rarely played with other boys and occasionally ran away to stay with neighbors in order to avoid his stepmother.

Jacob decided that he would go to the United States to pursue a better life. Letters from his brother Henry describing his life in New York City fueled Jacob's desire. At age 17, with two dollars in his pocket, Jacob set out to seek his fortune in the world. Fortunately, he took after his mother more than his father. She had been a devout, thrifty, hardworking woman who had started him on a lifelong habit of morning devotions. "Soon after I left the village," Astor later wrote, "I sat down beneath a tree to rest, and there I made three resolutions: to be honest, to be industrious, and not to gamble."

Firmly committed to those resolutions, he earned passage to London by working as an oarsman guiding a large raft of logs to market.

ON TO AMERICA

In 1780, when Jacob reached London, travel to the Americas was nearly impossible due to the war between the American colonists and Great Britain. While waiting for the conflict to end, Jacob joined his brother George, who worked in their uncle's London company, Astor and Broadwood. George helped Jacob get a job at the company, which manufactured and sold pianos and flutes.

Jacob used his time in England wisely. He worked long hours, studied the English language, and lived simply, saving almost all of his earnings. When the Revolutionary War came to an end in 1783, he was able to book passage for the United States with enough money left over to buy seven German flutes, which he hoped to sell at a profit in the New World.

Just outside the harbor of Baltimore, however, the ship became stuck in ice. During the weeks of boredom and frustration while Astor waited for the ice to break, he became friends with a fellow German immigrant who was making a handsome living in the fur trade. Astor listened eagerly to every detail as the man explained how he purchased furs from Indians and frontiersmen, packaged them, and sold them to large dealers. By March 1784, when Astor finally got ashore and made his way to New York, he could hardly wait to get into the fur business.

Astor thought it would be hard to learn English, but in six weeks he could speak his new language fairly well.

FUR MERCHANT

Realizing that he still had a lot to learn, Astor took a job at the store of fur merchant Robert Browne. With his passion for learning and his shrewd business sense, Astor quickly advanced from menial jobs, such as beating the moths out of stacks of furs, to the important post of fur buyer. In 1786, he figured he had learned enough to go into business for himself. Astor opened a shop on Queen Street in New York City and traveled all over the state buying skins.

Having learned from his old shipmate that furs were selling in London for as much as five times their cost in the United States, Astor bought space on a cargo ship and sailed with a load of furs to Great Britain. Ever concerned with efficiency, he arranged to take flutes, pianos, and violins from his uncle on the return voyage to New York. In addition to running his fur business, he became the first musical instrument dealer in the United States.

As his fur business grew more profitable, Astor expanded it. He obtained his own warehouses in Montreal and hired his own trappers. By 1793, Astor had become the largest supplier of furs in the U.S. Eventually, his fur-gathering empire stretched as far west as the coast of Oregon. He continued to live simply, residing with his family on Little Dock Street in a small house that served as his store until 1800, when he separated his home and business, moving with his family to a house on Broadway. His work was his life, and only rarely did he take time out for horseback riding or to attend the theater.

Around the same time he opened his first shop, Astor married Sarah Todd, who proved to be a valuable assistant with a good eye for business details. John Jacob and Sarah would eventually have seven children together, five of whom would survive beyond infancy: Magdalen, John Jacob III, William Backhouse, Dorothea, and Eliza.

In 1790, Astor moved his shop to Little Dock Street (later Water Street) to give both his growing business and his family more room.

By the turn of the century, Astor was wealthy enough to build his own ships to carry his furs to overseas markets. With his business expanding, he looked for new, lucrative markets, such as the Far East. Never one to let an opportunity slip away, he loaded his ships with silk and tea for the return voyages and made a huge profit on both ends of the trips. Business was so good that in 1808 Astor quietly became New York City's first millionaire.

SETBACKS AND SOLUTIONS

Not all was smooth sailing for Astor in his rise to wealth. In 1807, President Thomas Jefferson imposed an embargo (ban) on American export shipping in retaliation for British anti-American policies. Unfortunately, the embargo hurt U.S. merchants, who were far more dependent on trade with Great Britain than the British were on American trade. U.S. exports fell 80 percent that year, and its imports from other nations dropped by 60 percent. Those who depended on overseas shipping for their livelihood, such as Astor, were especially hard-hit.

Astor, however, was not the type of person to accept adversity meekly, and he was one of the few merchants to find a way around the embargo. He received Thomas Jefferson's special permission to allow an "esteemed citizen of China" to return to his homeland on one of Astor's ships. Once he got the permission, Astor loaded the ship with his goods. At a time when goods were scarce and prices high, he cleared $200,000 on the voyage, compared to an average profit of $30,000 on his voyages to China.

Although the Embargo Act of 1807 closed all U.S. ports to export shipping, strict enforcement of the act did not begin until 1808. Once the negative effects of the ban on the U.S. economy became clear, however, the Non-Intercourse Act was passed, allowing trade with nations other than Great Britain and France.

John Jacob Astor's shipping rivals accused him of finding a Chinese man somewhere on the New York docks and claiming he was a highly ranked Chinese official. Astor wrote a letter to a New York newspaper stating that if his rivals had knowledge of the facts of the case, they would see that everything was in order. He offered no further explanation, and the matter ended there.

Astor was not always so fortunate. In June 1811, some of his men had a run-in with Indians near his fur depot, Astoria, in Oregon. Astor's ship, the *Tonquin*, had sailed up the coast to buy furs and had stopped at an Indian village to do some trading. The Indians became angry with the men on the ship and attacked. During the skirmish, the *Tonquin* was destroyed. The disaster cost him over a million dollars, but Astor took the loss in stride. News of the

The Tonquin *was no stranger to misfortune. Earlier in 1811, it had sailed to establish Astor's trading post, Astoria, at the mouth of the Columbia River in Oregon. On March 25, eight crew members drowned while searching for a channel to allow them to cross the mouth of the Columbia.*

Astoria as it looked in 1813. After the War of 1812, possession of Astoria reverted from Britain to the United States, but Astor's rivals were firmly established near the fort. Astor asked for protection from the U.S. government to reoccupy Astoria, but nothing was ever done about his request.

incident did not dissuade him from attending the theater that night. When questioned about his apparent disregard, he responded, "What would you have me do? Would you have me stay at home and weep for what I could not help?"

Then, during the War of 1812, the British took possession of Astoria. Astor's employee in charge there—who was suspected of sympathizing with a rival trading company—surrendered the fort and its

valuable stock of furs without a fight. Astor's response was more emotionally involved that time. "Had our place and our property been fairly captured," Astor said, "I should have preferred it; I should not feel as if I were disgraced."

After the setbacks, Astor shifted his sights from fur and shipping to a single-minded interest that would consume the rest of his life: real estate.

ONE WAY TO GROW

Astor's interest in real estate had begun several decades earlier. In 1789, he purchased two lots and four half-lots on Manhattan Island from his brother Henry, who had invested the profits of his prosperous tavern in real estate. Over the years, Astor became convinced that Manhattan real estate was a potential bonanza. He saw that New York City was a magnet for new businesses and immigrants seeking their fortunes. From 1790 to 1800, the list of merchants operating in New York swelled from 248 to more than 1,100. Astor anticipated that the city's growth would continue until New York rivaled the greatest cities of Europe. In studying the geography of Manhattan, the center of New York's thriving economy, Astor saw that the city could expand in only one direction—north.

In the early 1800s, northern Manhattan was occupied primarily by old Dutch farms and English country estates. Astor's basic strategy was to invest a large portion of his fur and shipping earnings in relatively inexpensive, empty tracts of land north of the city. From 1800 to 1820, Astor invested more than

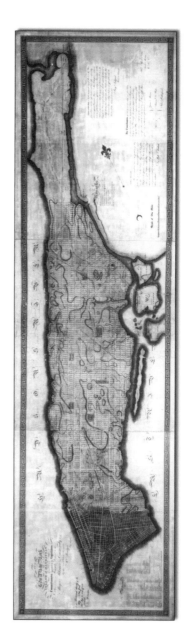

A map of Manhattan Island in 1811

$700,000 of his earnings in Manhattan real estate, and once he bought more than $200,000 worth of real estate in a single year. Thereafter, he financed the purchase of more land from the lease, sale, or rental of his other properties.

"LESS A BUILDER THAN A SPECULATOR"

Sticking to his vow of industriousness, Astor had worked very hard in his fur and shipping businesses.

A 1931 view of mid-town Manhattan, where Astor would make much of his fortune. Long after Astor died, Manhattan properties continued to be some of the most expensive real estate in the world.

He had arisen early, had usually begun work before 7:00 A.M., and had often worked into the evening, even in later years when his fortune was well established. When it came to the real-estate business, however, Astor let others do much of the work for him. In fact, he made the bulk of his money during the last 25 years of his life, when he had either severely cut back his work duties or retired altogether. According to authors Ric Burns and James Sanders, "Less a builder than a speculator, Astor did little to improve the properties he purchased, patiently waiting instead for the city to move north before selling his holdings at a breath-taking profit then buying still more land, even farther to the north."

Even on the properties he kept, he seldom initiated any building projects. Astor developed a system of offering 21-year leases to tenants for very low prices; the tenants would then take responsibility for development of the land. When the leases expired, ownership of the improvements would go to Astor. As the city steadily expanded toward these lands, they became ever more valuable to those wanting to establish themselves in the prestigious city. In 1826, the value of all Manhattan real estate was estimated at $64 million. A decade later, the figure had soared to $233 million.

As Astor immersed himself more deeply in these land dealings, "his interest in real estate grew more systematic, more ambitious, and more calculating," according to authors Edwin G. Burrows and Mike Wallace. By 1830, he had pulled out of the shipping business completely, and shortly thereafter he sold

Astor's system of making tenants responsible for developing the land they rented would be common practice in large cities across the United States by 1929.

"Nothing was trivial with [Astor] . . . and it is remarkable that he never embarked in any scheme until he had mastered its most trifling details. Few men have ever shown a deeper and more far-reaching knowledge of their profession and the issues involved in it than he."
—James D. McCabe Jr.,
Great Fortunes and How They Were Made

At his peak, Astor owned more than 300 separate parcels of land on Manhattan Island. Included in this was Eden Farm, which became the famous Times Square, shown here in 1923.

The only time Astor could recall being bested was when an elderly couple held on to their house on the block where Astor wished to build his hotel. Astor had no choice but to keep raising his offer. He ended up paying double what the house was worth.

his interest in the American Fur Company so that he could devote more time to his real-estate operations. On weekends, he would often ride his horse far into the countryside north of the city in search of promising land to buy.

The only time Astor initiated a building project on a grand scale was following his wife's death in 1834. He had observed a great deal of traffic in the area of Manhattan near city hall, and he decided that would be a good spot for a hotel. Astor chose to build the largest and finest that money could buy. He tore down his own house and all the other buildings on the block to make way for his 6-story, 309-room Park Hotel. It opened in 1836 and was soon renamed Astor House. While many people thought the building was impressive but not beautiful, the hotel's size and such luxurious touches as a menu that included 30 meat and fish dishes each day made it the nation's most famous hotel for nearly two decades.

COLD-BLOODED TACTICS

Astor was not a person who clamored for public attention. After his difficult, unsuccessful venture in establishing the fur-trading center of Astoria in 1811, Astor generally stayed in the background of his business dealings. This preference, together with his modest living habits, kept him out of the public spotlight for years.

But eventually, Astor's land holdings and personal fortune grew so great that people began taking a closer look at him. Some did not like what they saw,

Astor House, unlike many of the most elegant mansions of the time, had toilets and bathing facilities on every floor.

Shrewd Businessman

There was no doubt that Astor, who earned considerable fortunes in three vastly different types of enterprises—fur trading, shipping, and real estate—was an extraordinarily shrewd businessman. One of his most astute maneuvers caught New York state officials completely off guard. During the Revolutionary War, a wealthy Manhattan gentleman named Roger Morris had remained loyal to the king of England. When the British surrendered, Morris fled his estate, which New York confiscated and then sold to farmers.

Somehow, Astor learned that Morris had arranged his affairs so that he had only a life interest in the estate. In other words, he had taken legal steps to transfer his land to his heirs. The state could confiscate the land only during Morris's life; once he died, it reverted to the heirs. With Morris dead, Astor quietly bought out the claims of Morris's heirs and then informed the New York state government that the land belonged to him. New York fought Astor's claim in court, but the judges sided with Astor.

Now the state was in an awkward position. It either had to evict the farmers who had bought the land in good faith and established themselves there, or it had to negotiate some sort of settlement with Astor. Astor eventually walked away with half a million dollars—a profit of more than $450,000—in exchange for dropping his claims.

either on a personal level or in business. The poor German immigrant never developed the refined sense of culture that the elite of New York City expected. According to Burns and Sanders, "Astor stunned the city's polite society with his appalling manners—mixing peas and ice cream, then eating them with a knife, then wiping his hands on the tablecloth."

Even though Astor held rigidly to the vow of integrity he had made upon leaving Germany and was scrupulously honest in all his dealings, his business methods brought him disrepute, as well. He was accused of being "utterly devoid of generosity." He was stingy in paying his employees. Some saw Astor as inclined, as the years went on, to take advantage of others' misery.

When the panic of 1837 caused great economic hardship for many people, Astor picked up numerous properties for less than they would have been worth in better economic times. Astor also foreclosed on property owners who couldn't make their mortgage payments. Astor regularly bought up mortgages of struggling farmers or acquired them through loans and then foreclosed on them and obtained the property for next to nothing. In 1837, he initiated 60 foreclosure proceedings.

Even when he was frail and sickly, Astor did not regret his cutthroat business practices. One of the

Although Astor did not pay his employees well, he inspired in them "a zeal in his service that made them willing to undertake anything . . . for him."

mortgage: a temporary pledge of property to a creditor until a loan is paid back

A view of City Hall (center) between Broadway (left) and Chatham Streets in 1822. John Jacob Astor lived on Broadway for much of his life.

last actions in his career was the foreclosure of another mortgage. Just weeks before his death on March 29, 1848, he appeared to regret that he had not been even more aggressive in his dealings. "Could I begin life again, knowing what I now know, and had the money to invest," he confided to a friend, "I would buy every square foot of land on the island of Manhattan."

LEGACY

Astor left most of his incredible fortune to his son William and gave smaller portions to his hometown of Waldorf and several different charities. He also gave the city of New York a $400,000 endowment to set up a library, which reigned for years as the best reference library in the country.

An engraving showing the front view of the Astor Library

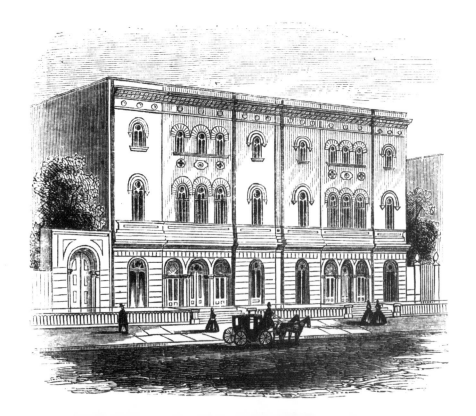

Astor's failure to give more of his fortune to New York provoked some venomous responses. Many people despised Astor and claimed that his fortune had been created by the citizens of New York. James Gordon Bennett of the *New York Herald* argued that at least half Astor's fortune belonged to New York City. "During the last fifty years . . . his property has been augmented in value by the aggregate intelligence, industry, enterprise and commerce of New York," wrote Bennett. "But instead of [giving half his fortune to New York City] he has only left less than half a million for a public library. . . ."

Astor demonstrated the immense riches that were possible in real estate. Although many others had tried to get rich on the strategy of buying land and waiting for it to gain value, Astor was the first person to make it work on a huge scale. He foresaw the tremendous growth of New York City and laid out a systematic plan to make money off that growth.

Over the course of his career, Astor invested roughly $2 million in real estate. Not only did he profit from the sale of land as the city expanded, but he also accumulated 7,200 properties on which he collected rent. By the time of his death, that property was worth more than $20 million. This made him the richest person in the United States, with assets more than double that of the second wealthiest. Astor's investments continued to pay off for his heirs as New York developed into the major business center of the world. By 1900, the value of his investments was estimated at more than $450 million.

William Backhouse Astor (1792-1875), John Jacob Astor's second son, inherited much of his father's fortune. William adopted his father's business practices and left his heirs with an increased fortune. Many of John Jacob Astor's descendants would become prominent in their own right.

3

WILLIAM LEVITT

LEVITTOWN AND THE SHAPING OF SUBURBIA

At the end of World War II, the United States faced a severe housing shortage. Millions of war veterans had returned from active duty overseas only to find there simply were no houses available, especially not for people with such meager savings as the average soldier. Young men who had sacrificed years of their lives and suffered through the horrors of war in the service of their country were living in shameful shacks or crowding in with relatives—if they could find any place at all.

The man who solved the postwar housing problem was a New York contractor named William Levitt. In the course of developing a way to mass-produce affordable yet sturdy houses, Levitt created a side effect that has had mixed results for the

William Levitt (1907-1994) revolutionized the building industry by using assembly line techniques to mass-produce houses. In doing this, he created the first suburb, Levittown, which provoked a storm of criticism, in addition to being imitated repeatedly.

American landscape—the middle-class suburb. While the idea of building residential communities on the more peaceful outskirts of large cities dates back thousands of years to the ancient Egyptians, Levitt pioneered a major shift to suburban living as the dominant middle-class lifestyle in the postwar United States.

ESCAPE FROM THE CITY

Levitt made no apologies for drawing Americans away from the bustle of city life. "I have a friend who goes into rhapsodies over cities and all the joys he gets from them," Levitt once noted. "Well, I don't understand it."

William Jaird Levitt's distaste for cities came from early childhood experience. He spent the first part of his youth in the New York City borough of Brooklyn, where he was born on February 11, 1907, to Abraham and Pauline Levitt. Abraham Levitt was an attorney who liked to practice his persuasive arguments at home as much as in the courtroom. He spent many evenings giving Bill and his younger brother, Alfred, his opinions on everything from politics to art to the Brooklyn Dodgers baseball team. Among his strongly held opinions was that the value of their house would go down if blacks moved into homes in their neighborhood. When a young black professional bought a house on his street, Abraham Levitt promptly moved out toward the outskirts of the city. Throughout his life, Bill never considered moving back to the congested inner city; he always preferred to be outside the city.

William Levitt's parents, Abraham and Pauline Levitt

The Construction Business

Abraham (center), Alfred (right), and William Levitt

Bill, who had always disliked school, dropped out of New York University after his junior year without a career goal in mind. He worked at a variety of jobs, none of which held his interest for long. While Bill was in this drifting state, his father grew frustrated at his inability to sell a lot that he owned and no longer wanted. In the late 1920s, Bill and his father decided that they might have better luck selling if there was a good house on the lot. Alfred, whose main interest was art, also quit school and joined the project. He drew up the plans, while Bill and Abraham supervised the building.

Sure enough, the Levitts were able to sell the house, and the profit they made encouraged the brothers to go into home construction as a career.

In late 1929, Bill Levitt married Rhoda Kirshner. The couple had two sons, William and James. Levitt would later be divorced and remarried twice.

57

As Levitt & Sons, Inc.—with Alfred creating the building designs and Bill in charge of construction and sales—the Levitt brothers built and sold 600 houses over the next four years.

The Levitts did not range far from their neighborhood in Long Island, New York, where, ironically, they rented rather than owned their own homes. As they grew more successful, they began to seek out larger projects, targeting families who worked in the New York metropolitan area but wanted to live in the more spacious suburbs. In 1934, the Levitt brothers built an entire subdivision—the 200-house Strathmore-at-Manhasset development on Long Island. Establishing a reputation as quality builders of individually crafted houses for the upper-middle class, the Levitts kept expanding their work force. From 1935 to 1942, their company built and sold more than 2,000 houses.

Mass-Produced Houses

As the United States became more involved in World War II, there was a sudden need for low-cost housing to accommodate the millions of people moving to military installations, or permanent bases. The Levitts responded by throwing together a "quick-and-dirty" housing development near Norfolk, Virginia. In order to get the houses up as fast as possible, they laid long strips of concrete as if they were building a street. Then they put up one wooden-frame house after another on the concrete—1,600 in all. The project proved a disaster. The bleak string of cookie-cutter houses was so unattractive that, even with the high demand for basic shelter, the Levitts could not sell the houses. Many of them stood empty.

Rather than wash their hands of the whole low-income housing business, the Levitts learned from their mistakes. They figured out ways to cut costs and build quickly without sacrificing quality. As a result, their next project, the development of more than 750 basic houses for enlisted men joining the U.S. Navy in the same Norfolk area, was a success.

This experience inspired Bill Levitt to study ways of mass-producing quality, low-priced houses. He realized that this would never work using the traditional house construction methods that had been virtually unchanged for centuries. If automobiles were built the way houses were, with a few workers performing all the steps to custom-build each car just the way the buyer dictated, the cost would be so high that few people would be able to afford them. It was Henry Ford's assembly line, in which specialists rapidly performed the same job on each vehicle, that had made cars affordable for the average person. Levitt saw that the trick to mass-producing houses was to get the same type of system in place. But since a house was too big to move along an assembly belt, Levitt had to create a situation in which, as he put it, "instead of the product going on an assembly line, the product stood still and the mechanics moved."

Levitt's plans for mass-produced housing had to be put on hold for a while when, in 1943, he joined the Seabees, a unit responsible for handling engineering tasks for the United States Navy. But when

Levitt in his naval uniform, as a Seabee. "Seabee" comes from the initials C.B., which are short for Construction Battalion. The Seabees built military facilities, such as harbors and airfields, during World War II.

he returned to civilian life at the war's end in 1945, the time was ripe for putting his plans into action. Residential housing construction had come to a standstill during the war as soldiers left the country for overseas duty and industry concentrated on producing war materials. Now, suddenly, 13 million military personnel were returning to civilian life, producing a terrible housing shortage.

LAYING THE GROUNDWORK FOR LEVITTOWN

Levitt saw that his ideas on mass-producing houses could solve a serious national problem as well as provide him with a good living. He began buying hundreds of acres of flat potato fields near the town of Hicksville on Long Island in preparation for a new housing project on a scale greater than anyone had ever imagined. In 1946, his company resumed its prewar business of custom home-building and constructed 1,000 houses, while Levitt quietly bought up all the land he needed for the new small city that he and Alfred planned to build. At first, the brothers considered holding a contest to choose the name for this new development, but in the end they named it after themselves—Levittown.

Only one obstacle remained before Levitt could put his plan into motion—financing. Levitt's company did not have millions of dollars of cash on hand to pay for all the start-up costs of building this community. Most war veterans did not have enough money for a down payment even on the low-cost houses Levitt planned to build. Banks could not afford to take the huge risk of lending money to builders on speculation or to first-time home buyers without some guarantee that they could get their money back if builders and buyers failed to meet their obligations. At Levitt's urging, the federal government decided to step in and provide a financial safety net. The Federal Housing Authority (FHA) arranged easy terms for builders to borrow money for housing projects. At the same time, it agreed to guarantee lenders the entire amount of the mortgage for veterans so that they would not even have to come up with a down payment.

With government support in place, Levitt was ready to go all out on his revolutionary building

Levitt worked with the FHA to set up a plan for lending money to veterans for housing. He told the FHA commissioner, "the only way we [are] going to get a volume of housing [is] to grant to the veteran, in effect, a 100 percent mortgage." The FHA also guaranteed 95 percent for qualified non-veterans if the buyer put down 5 percent.

binge. "The dice were loaded," he said. "We had known all along we could mass-produce houses if there was a market for them and credit for builders. Now the market was there and the government was ready with the backing. How could we lose?"

"It Was As If They Fell to Earth"

Levitt had carefully analyzed the entire house construction process and had broken it down into 26 separate steps. He then trained specialized workers in each of the 26 steps. Determined to keep the cost of the houses affordable without cutting corners on quality, he constantly sought ways to trim expenses. Levitt refused to use expensive union labor. He was willing to try new labor-saving devices such as paint-sprayers. When nails were in short supply and prices rose, he started a plant to manufacture his own nails. For those supplies he could not manufacture himself, he insisted on buying direct from the factory so that he could avoid paying fees to the middleman.

Levitt hired 80 subcontractors to build Levittown according to his plans. The construction system he put in place astounded observers with its efficiency. The first crew arrived at a site, where they dug a narrow, 4-foot trench outlining the future 25-by-32-foot house. Within 15 minutes, they moved on to the next lot, where they would repeat the procedure. They would be followed by cement trucks that laid one foundation after another.

Trucks would drive up and down the empty streets, dropping identical loads of lumber, bricks,

Labor unions protested Levitt's refusal to use their workers. Once, when a union was picketing Levitt, a man left the line to look at a Levitt house. He eventually bought one.

As builders fueled by the FHA loans rushed to construct new houses, lumber grew scarce and expensive. Levitt, however, had the foresight to buy his own timber lands in the western United States, as well as his own lumber mills, to keep him supplied.

pipes, nails, and other building materials on one lot after another. They were followed by a series of specialized crews, each performing a different task— laying bricks, raising studs, hammering the floor into place, installing pipes or electrical wires, building walls, painting, and other construction jobs. When they finished their work at one site, they rushed on to the next and repeated the job. Production bonuses encouraged all workers to get as much done as they could without sacrificing quality. At its peak, the Levitts' construction company built an average of 35 houses a day. The houses popped up so quickly

Levitt's team of workers assembling house frames during the construction of Levittown

The Cape Cod, several of which are shown here, was a popular, basic style of house in Levittown.

that one author marveled, "It was as if they fell to earth instead of growing from it."

The typical Levittown house was a one-and-a-half-story structure with no basement. It held a 12-by-16-foot living room, two bedrooms, a kitchen, and a bathroom all on the first floor. Above this was an attic that could be converted to two more bedrooms and a bathroom.

With the FHA requiring no money down for veterans, and house payments at only $56 per month, the deal was too appealing for buyers to pass up.

A Levittown patio and a typical Levittown living room inside a Cape Cod-style house

Levitt's sales staff had no trouble attracting customers. It did not matter that Levittown had absolutely no jobs or industry to entice new residents. More than 80 percent of those who bought houses already had jobs in New York City's business district, which was within reasonable driving distance of Levittown. In a single week, the company sold 350 houses just to walk-in customers at its Levittown store, where it had some of its building materials on display. Before long, thousands of middle-income people were lining up day and night for a chance to buy their own houses. Levitt gave priority to veterans. In 1950, he sold 5,500 houses in Levittown as well as another 400 in a separate Long Island project. Levittown eventually filled to capacity with a population of more than 70,000.

MORE THAN JUST A CONTRACTOR

Bill Levitt was a brash, outspoken man who took pride in holding contrary opinions, saying such things as, "I hate all forms of exercise." He was so confrontational that his brother, Alfred, left the company in the 1950s in exasperation over dealing with him. Still, Bill Levitt put a lot of thoughtful planning into the Levittown community, dividing it into sections and providing each with schools, parks, recreational facilities, and shopping centers. As an added convenience to customers, the houses came complete with a refrigerator, a stove, a washing machine, a fireplace, and, as its popularity increased, a television. Levitt packaged all of this into the low price of $6,990.

Despite his well-known stubbornness, Levitt listened to his customers even when he disagreed with them. One prospective buyer complained about the three-burner stoves that Levitt had installed in all houses. He disputed Levitt's explanation that four-burner stoves took up too much space. Trying to end the argument, Levitt finally told the customer that if he could find a four-burner stove that took up no more room than a three-burner, Levitt would buy it. To his surprise, the customer did just that.

Levitt made sure Levittown had plenty of things to do and places to go, including several swimming pools.

True to his word, Levitt canceled an order for 1,000 stoves and bought four-burners instead.

Levitt's attention to detail and quality paid off. His homes proved to be solidly constructed, and they held up well over the years. "He did a great thing for us veterans," said one Levittown buyer. "He did it well and he could have got a lot more money for it than he did."

SUBURBAN CONFORMITY

In the words of author Ron Rosenbaum, "Once Bill Levitt showed fellow builders how to mass-produce entire communities, how to do for housing what Henry Ford did for cars, America went on a non-stop burb-building binge." With such an enormous backup of housing demand and the government's generous terms for builders, contractors all over the nation copied Levitt's methods and mass-produced thousands of instant suburban communities.

Critics looked upon this new middle-class lifestyle with a mixture of horror and disdain. Of grave concern was the fact that Levitt's assembly line system required that the houses be virtually identical, with only a few variations of style. With its row after row of identical-looking houses, Levittown struck some people as a place so sterile that no glimmer of creativity or individualism remained. Even Levitt himself confessed to occasionally getting lost amid the uniform streets and houses. The rigid regulations that he imposed on the Levittown community, such as the ban on fences and the requirement that

"You could go literally miles in any direction without reaching the end of these impassive rows of little houses."
—*Life* magazine

lawns be cut once a week, only added to the cold impersonality of the commuter suburb.

To a large degree, Levittown was able to overcome its reputation as a huge collection of sterile wooden boxes because of the individuality of its buyers. With such small mortgages, many buyers were able to pay for their houses within a few years. Rather than move somewhere more expensive, they used their extra money to build their own additions, make improvements, and redo the landscaping, until each house took on its own unique appearance.

Another criticism of Levitt was that while he freely took credit for putting housing within reach of the average American, there were many Americans he purposely excluded. The families were as uniform as the initial housing. Almost all were young families with small children. "Everyone is so young that sometimes it's hard to remember how to get along with older people," one resident admitted.

Even more glaring was the uniformity of race. Reflecting the prejudice of the time, Levitt would not allow blacks to move to Levittown at all during the 1950s. Levitt excused this as a business necessity that overrode any moral obligations. "As a Jew, I have no room in my mind or heart for racial prejudice," he said. "But . . . I have come to know that if we sell one house to a Negro family, then 90 to 95 percent of our white customers will not buy into the community. That is their attitude, not ours. . . . We can solve a housing problem, or we can try to solve a racial problem. But we cannot combine the two."

If a lawn in Levittown was not mowed once a week, Levitt would send someone to mow it and then send the bill to the homeowner.

In 1963, civil-rights demonstrations were held at a Levitt development in Maryland in protest against Levitt's all-white policy.

LEGACY

At the height of his building success, Levitt proudly called his company "the General Motors of the construction industry." He never did reach that type of dominance in construction, however, and his influence as a developer ebbed with the passage of years.

Levitt eventually sold his company for $92 million, but he spent so extravagantly that when he died in 1994, he was bankrupt.

To his credit, Levitt helped fill a desperate housing shortage. Without his pioneering of mass-production building techniques and his experimental development of Levittown, hundreds of thousands of people would have been living in substandard housing for years. Levitt began to consider affordable housing his mission in life.

Toward the end of his career, Levitt tried, with mixed success, to adapt his mass-production construction methods to third-world countries such as Nigeria, Venezuela, and Iran, where affordable housing was desperately needed. His final project, the Levittshahr development in Iran, could not proceed when an anti-American Islamic revolution swept the existing government from power.

The mass-production of housing, meanwhile, has fallen into disfavor, largely due to objections to the bland uniformity that characterized Levittown. Today's housing construction has largely reverted to the expensive custom-building of the past.

Levitt's role in shaping the modern American suburb is probably more far-reaching and certainly more controversial than his influence on building practices. Although the development of a suburban lifestyle was inevitable, given the freedom of transportation allowed by the automobile, Levittown provided a prototype for a community that would supply comfortable housing for middle-class people who commute to work elsewhere. Debate continues to rage over whether this has had an overall positive or negative effect on society. Critics continue to scorn Levittown as a symbol of sterile middle-class conformity. The flight of middle-class whites from the cities to overwhelmingly white suburbs hurt the cities, on which the suburbanites continued to depend for their livelihood, and increased the racial divide in the country. On the other hand, Americans have shown a clear preference for the less crowded, more orderly way of life the suburbs offer, a lifestyle that William Levitt helped bring into existence.

An aerial view of Levittown's rows of houses

4

DEL WEBB

SUN CITY:
THE RETIREMENT OASIS

Del Webb's first career was over before it really got started. His lifelong hope of playing major-league baseball ended in 1925, when he tore a ligament in his knee while sliding into home. Any thoughts he might have had about rehabilitating the knee and getting back to the ballpark were dashed when he contracted typhoid fever. Webb survived the illness, but not before it wasted his 200-pound frame to just 99 pounds.

Webb eventually regained his strength, but he decided not to go back to baseball. Still, he had trouble finding a replacement for his dream. He was a good carpenter, and for a time he drifted from one construction job to the next with no particular career goals in mind.

In developing the first community that catered specifically and exclusively to the elderly, Del Webb (1899-1974) helped revolutionize many Americans' ideas about retirement.

Del Webb pitched for several minor-league teams before he contracted typhoid.

Del Webb hated being called Delbert.

In 1928, he took a job with a small contractor in Phoenix, Arizona, who was in charge of constructing a grocery store. The contractor went broke and disappeared without finishing the job. Webb decided to move on and look for work elsewhere, only to find that his last check from the contractor bounced. Hoping the grocery owner might pay him for his work, Webb complained to him. Upset at being left with an unfinished store, the owner made a proposal that could solve both their problems: he offered to hire Webb to finish the job.

Webb agreed. The work went so well that he gained the confidence to start his own construction company. The negligence of that Phoenix contractor would one day affect the lives of thousands of elderly Americans. When Del Webb carved a brand-new community out of the Arizona desert, he changed the whole idea of retirement.

UNDERCOVER BASEBALL STAR

Delbert Eugene Webb was born in Fresno, California, in 1899, to a family with a long history of hard work in the area of building. He was the grandson of a German farmer responsible for installing one of California's first irrigation systems. His father was an independent building contractor.

Del learned both carpentry and baseball from his father, who played in amateur baseball leagues. Del was more interested in baseball by far. The family's prosperous times ended in 1913, when Del's father went bankrupt in the unstable business of contracting. Two years later, at age 16, Del quit school and left home to make his own way in the world. "I've been on the move ever since," he later said.

Standing six feet four inches tall and weighing 200 pounds, Del was a strong and gifted athlete. Pursuing his dream of playing professional ball, he played for amateur teams on weekends and worked as a carpenter during the week. This was not easy, because he had to hide the evidence from some very strict aunts who kept close tabs on their nephew's life. "They thought baseball was trafficking with the devil, so when I finally went off to play, I had to do it now and then under an assumed name," he recalled.

When the United States became involved in World War I in 1917, Webb found steady work in the Oakland, California, shipyards. In 1919, after the end of the war, he married his childhood sweetheart, Hazel Church, and pressed on with his baseball career. He traveled up and down the West Coast from Mexico to Canada, hurling his fastball for minor-league teams while making ends meet with temporary carpentry work. But when the knee injury and typhoid fever struck, Webb decided to move to the dry, hot air of Phoenix in order to recuperate.

> "Those old ladies [his aunts] were so religious they squeaked. I had to go to Sunday school and church, and . . . I wanted to play ball."
> —Del Webb

Del Webb married Hazel Church in 1919. She often helped him in the office in later years. Their marriage ended in 1952, and Del Webb would remarry in 1961.

BUILDING A CONSTRUCTION BUSINESS

Webb's accidental entry into the construction business paid off. Not only was he a competent builder who gained a reputation for completing projects on time and under budget, but he also found he possessed social skills that aided him tremendously. Webb was an outgoing man who was superb at selling to strangers and had a flair for making friends in high places. Gaining the confidence of such people as multimillionaire Howard Hughes, hotel giant Conrad Hilton, and President Franklin Roosevelt helped him win entry to the bidding competition for important projects. By 1935, Webb's small company was doing $3 million of business a year.

Fort Huachuca had originally protected early settlers of Arizona from Apache Indians. In 1942, Webb's buildings would serve the U.S. Army as World War II progressed.

World War II sent a flurry of urgent government construction projects Webb's way. He built airfields and military installations, including the sprawling Fort Huachuca army base in Arizona, which his

company completed in three months. The company also took only three weeks to assemble a 10,000-person camp in California where the suspicious U.S. government confined Japanese-Americans during the war.

Webb was such a reliable contractor that the military kept sending him business even after the war ended in 1945. Webb put up more air bases and missile complexes, as well as facilities for the space program. At the same time, the adventurous contractor tested the waters in a variety of civilian projects, such as shopping centers and hotels.

Webb was a master salesman who began to spend more and more of his time on the road, winning new clients. Eventually, he reserved permanent hotel suites in Phoenix, New York, and Beverly Hills, which he used as bases of operations, and he kept business suits in half a dozen other strategically located hotels. A great believer in entertaining potential clients, he took out memberships in 14 country clubs around the U.S.

Perhaps Webb's most striking business trait was his thirst for publicity. LaVergne "Jake" Jacobson, who started out as a carpenter during Webb's first construction projects and worked his way up to company president, once observed of Webb, "He's got quite an ego. . . . He likes to see his name on top of buildings." Not only did Webb include his full name in naming his business the Del E. Webb Corporation, but he included his picture in most of his advertising.

In the 1940s, Webb managed to get himself far more publicity than any other contractor of his size

Webb had definite ideas about how to run his business, and he was not one to compromise. One employee found out the hard way that Webb was serious about standardizing operations. Webb insisted that those who worked for him would drive black cars. Ignoring the regulation, the employee drove his tan car to work. At the end of the day, he discovered that Webb had ordered it removed from the parking lot and painted black while the man was at work.

Del Webb swinging a bat with Joe DiMaggio (1914-1999), one of the most famous baseball players in history. DiMaggio played for the Yankees while Webb was an owner.

in the nation. In 1945, he joined Dan Topping and Larry McPhail to purchase baseball's most famous team, the New York Yankees. For two decades, Del made a point of listing that ownership in his advertising and sales pitches. In 1946, he achieved notoriety of a different sort by building the Flamingo, the first luxury casino in Las Vegas, for reputed mobster Bugsy Siegel.

INTO REAL ESTATE

Although Webb was making millions, he knew from his father's painful experience that construction was a fickle business. Today's building boom could quickly turn into a bust that would rock his company to its very core. Taking the advice of Jake Jacobson, he began steering the company into real-estate investments during the 1950s.

One construction project in Phoenix showed him that owning buildings could be far more lucrative than constructing them. Webb had originally intended to charge his standard $100,000 fee for constructing a shopping center. But instead, he asked for shares of ownership in the shopping center as payment. The rents paid by shopping center tenants brought him $80,000 a year for seven years. When Webb then sold his interest in the shopping center for $1 million, that gave him 15 times the profit that he would have earned had he simply accepted a construction fee.

Webb then invested heavily in land development. He bought large sections of cheap land in Arizona, Florida, California, and New Mexico, and set his construction company to work on building projects that increased the value of the land. Before long, Webb was building shopping plazas, hotels, and high-rise offices in Los Angeles, California; Tampa, Florida; Albuquerque, New Mexico; and Phoenix and Tucson, Arizona.

His most ambitious project was a joint venture with the Humble Oil Company. The U.S. government was preparing to move its National Aeronautics and Space Administration (NASA) headquarters from Florida to Houston in 1962. Anticipating the influx of thousands of space program employees, Webb and Humble drew up plans to build a new community for 25,000 people on 30,000 acres of land between Houston and Galveston. The two companies spent $25 million establishing facilities such as churches, apartments, and shopping centers to make the area attractive to the prospective buyers. The companies committed $200 million to the total development costs of the project.

RETIREMENT COMMUNITY

One of Webb's properties consisted of about 30,000 acres in the Arizona desert, 12 miles northeast of Phoenix. The land was empty except for some cotton fields and lettuce patches. Before Webb had quite decided what to do with the property, an unusual town just down the road from this land attracted his attention. In 1954, a rival Phoenix developer had begun to build the small community of Youngtown, a place that catered exclusively to retired people.

The more he thought about Youngtown, the more Webb suspected his rival was on to something big. The developer had put little thought or effort into Youngtown; the place had no special facilities for elderly people. Yet even without a major marketing campaign, retirees were rapidly buying homes in Youngtown.

Webb came to believe that retired people were a vastly underserved market. The United States had changed from a stationary rural society in which older people remained on the farm with their families after retirement age to a highly mobile urban society that had not really established a place for the elderly. Webb figured that if he could determine

A Russian immigrant named Ben Schleifer was the man behind the idea for Youngtown. The small city began as merely a group of houses and a store.

the living conditions that most appealed to retired people, he could turn his desert land into a popular residential community. Not only would he be able to make many millions of dollars on the deal, but he would also be providing a valuable service to retirees. Webb assigned one of his senior executives, Thomas Breen, to head the project.

WHAT DO ELDERLY PEOPLE WANT?

The plan carried with it a high risk. Most sociologists claimed that retired people wanted to be among the general population, that they enjoyed a mix of ages. According to the experts, the elderly had a great need to be productive members of mainstream society, and they would balk at severing ties with that society to live in isolation with other elderly people. This prevailing view was so strong that, according to Breen, "when we started this there wasn't one builder I talked to who didn't say I was out of my . . . mind."

But Webb's many years in business had taught him the importance of listening to the customers. Before jumping into the project, his researchers conducted many surveys to see what retirees really thought. "One thing we found was that almost everything ever written on the subject was a lot of baloney," said Breen. There turned out to be a large segment of retirees who were simply tired of the day-to-day struggle to adapt to an ever-changing society. They had a strong fear of being a burden on their families. They wanted to stay active but also wanted to lead their own lives, free from the hassles

Two of Del Webb's top executives: Tom Breen (right), who conducted research for Sun City, and Joe Ashton

Del Webb had actually hired another company to conduct the city-naming contest for him, but when Webb walked in on the review of the entries and said, "I like Sun City," his top executives knew that no one could argue. Jake Jacobson told the other company, "If Del Webb says that is the name, that's what it will be."

The construction of houses in Sun City progressed rapidly when the community first opened.

of other people's problems, including the challenge of dealing with small children.

From this market research, the Del E. Webb Corporation decided to go ahead with creating a retirement development restricted to people 50 years and older. There would be no schools and no children allowed. In 1959, Webb held a contest to name this new community and selected "Sun City" as the winning entry.

Rather than try to entice people to a desert with promises of a paradise, Webb decided to build the paradise first. Before he built or sold many houses, he invested a huge amount of money in constructing a large shopping center and a medical building. He

A golf course in Sun City

made the city more attractive by planting thousands of California palm trees and creating a 33-acre lake. "My grandfather, Jimmy Webb, used to grouch about being old," Webb noted. "Well, it's pretty grim, being old with nothing to do." Webb made sure there was plenty to do. He built golf courses that offered reduced rates for residents. He constructed a large community center in the center of town and a swimming pool. With these facilities in place, he then set about to sell older people on the idea of "active retirement." In Sun City, retirees could choose among dozens of recreational and club activities, but there would be no pressure on the residents to do anything.

At the opening of Sun City in 1960, interested retirees crowded the streets.

SUN CITY GROWS

In 1960, Webb began selling homes in Sun City, but what he was really selling was the idea of a fun, active, worry-free lifestyle. The response was even greater than the market research had predicted. On the very first weekend, Webb sold 237 homes. Dirt flew constantly as Webb's construction company built one-story, white-roofed, pastel-colored homes in 36 different models for new arrivals.

Webb's long-term strategy for making Sun City work required salesmen to file a detailed report about each buyer. This constant monitoring had two purposes. First, Webb wanted to find out what sort of people were buying houses in Sun City so that he could target advertising to people with similar interests and backgrounds. He soon discovered that most new residents were from the Midwest, so he focused his sales efforts in that area.

Second, Webb wanted to make sure that Sun City was meeting the needs and desires of its new residents. He figured that if he did everything possible to make his first residents happy, they would brag about the place to their friends and relatives, who would then be interested in buying homes in Sun City. (In effect, he would have created an unpaid sales force of thousands.) Sure enough, in the early years of Sun City, between one-third and one-half of those who bought homes had first heard about the place from friends who were already there.

By the end of 1962, the city was already half-filled, with a population of more than 7,000. Believing he was on the cutting edge of a new trend

Retirees play shuffleboard in Sun City.

An aerial view of the original Sun City, Arizona

in society, Webb quickly sought to expand his concept onto other properties he owned. Plans for Sun City, California, and Sun City, Florida, were quickly put into motion. Webb bought 3,000 acres of ranchland adjacent to Sun City, Arizona, to prepare for expansion once all the current lots were sold. The Del E. Webb Corporation was thriving, so Webb felt he could relax. He retired from the day-to-day operations of the company, although his name and picture were still featured prominently in sales promotions.

THE BRINK OF BANKRUPTCY

In 1965, however, real-estate values sagged in many areas of the nation. Sales of Webb's retirement community homes slowed, especially in the new California and Florida developments. Efforts to make temporary money on his Sun City, Arizona, expansion land by farming failed miserably. Webb was caught in a vulnerable position when disaster struck in Houston. Congress cut NASA's budget, which made the Houston housing project extremely risky. Suddenly, the Webb corporation had little income with which to pay off the tremendous debt on its vast land holdings.

A very worried Del Webb resumed control of his business and worked frantically to pull it out of its tailspin. The company had to back out of the Houston venture and sell out to Humble for what it could get. Land in California and office properties in Los Angeles had to be sold at disappointing prices. Webb even had to dump the expansion land near Sun City, Arizona, at a loss and sell his interest in the New York Yankees.

None of this would have been enough to save Webb's corporation from bankruptcy, however, were it not for a single fortunate business decision. In the early 1960s, the company had invested heavily in Nevada casinos, and the enormous profit these earned nursed the business through the lean years. By the end of the decade, Webb was back on his feet and expanding promotion of his retirement communities, including the creation of Sun City West, just up the road from the original Sun City.

LEGACY

Del Webb was a master salesman and a hard-driving businessman who made a handsome fortune, much of it in real-estate projects. By the time of his death

Another branch of Sun City, in Tucson, Arizona

in 1974, Webb had accumulated an estimated $50 million in assets. His company, which had grown into a $300-million-per-year business, has continued to prosper into the year 2002.

Webb's most lasting legacy is the existence of the "active life" retirement community. The company's description of Sun City, Arizona, as "the town that changed America's viewpoint on retirement" may be an exaggeration. Sun City has drawn its share of criticism for such things as its exclusion of minority groups and for catering to what some disgruntled former residents describe as a self-centered existence. The vast majority of retired Americans do not live in retirement communities.

Yet Webb did provide an alternative living arrangement that has appealed to and satisfied a significant number of elderly people. His real-estate developments in Sun City and Sun City West now house more than 70,000 people over the age of 50 and have spawned many imitation retirement projects.

"When I see what we've built, it's the most satisfying thing that's ever happened to me," said Del Webb, when asked about the significance of his real-estate career. "An old fellow came up to me once with tears in his eyes and thanked me for building Sun City."

Del Webb (far left) greets Sun City tenants. Many retirees have appreciated Webb's hard work in creating a community for them.

5

WALT DISNEY

WALT DISNEY WORLD RESORT: THE SECRET FLORIDA DEAL

During the summer of 1964, realtors in central Florida became aware that something strange was taking place near the small city of Orlando. Land seemed to be changing hands at an incredible rate for no apparent reason.

The more that curious people looked into the matter, the more suspicious it appeared. The land was all being purchased by wealthy, unknown buyers from out of state, who were going to great lengths to conceal their identities. They made it a condition of the sales that the landowners could reveal neither the identities of the buyers nor any of the details of the sale, including the price they received.

In the course of creating the world's most well-known entertainment empire, Walt Disney (1901-1966) orchestrated a huge, totally secret real-estate deal that changed the face of Florida.

News reporters tried everything they could think of to solve the riddle of the mystery buyers, without success. Even when they learned the names of some of the negotiators, they discovered that the out-of-state investors were using false names. The sales continued until more than 27,000 acres were in the hands of the mystery buyers.

No one could imagine what anyone would want with such a large chunk of forest, swamps, and farm-land so far from any established urban centers. Orlando was so unexceptional that its main claim to fame was that it was the spring training home of the Minnesota Twins baseball team.

Rumors began flying about who was making these deals. Some believed that the buyers were agents of the U.S. government in charge of a secret project to build a new complex to produce nuclear weapons. Others believed they were representatives of a large corporation, such as the Ford Motor Company, or one of the large airplane manufacturers, such as Boeing, looking to build a massive new plant. Some alert observers noted that entertainment industry giant Walt Disney had flown into the area twice in recent months. But then others noted that Disney's parents had been married near DeLand, just north of Orlando, so he had ties to the area.

It turned out that Disney *was* the man behind the great Florida land acquisition. Although far better known as an animated film pioneer and the creator of Mickey Mouse, Disney managed to pull off one of the largest and most fascinating real-estate deals of the twentieth century.

CHILDHOOD ON THE MOVE

Walter Elias Disney was born on December 5, 1901, in Chicago, Illinois. His father, Elias, worked as a carpenter and smalltime contractor. His mother, Flora, drew construction plans for Elias and raised their five children. Elias was a restless man who grew tired of city life. In 1906, he suddenly switched careers and moved the family to a 45-acre farm near Marceline, Missouri.

Walt later remembered his farm days as the most contented time of his life, a feeling that had much to do with the fact that he was too young to be expected to help with many of the chores. A stubborn man who refused to use fertilizers, Elias Disney spent four backbreaking years trying to succeed at farming.

Walt Disney's parents, Elias and Flora Disney

In 1910, when typhoid fever limited his ability to work, he finally gave up and put the farm up for auction.

The Disneys moved to Kansas City, where Elias worked as a newspaper distributor. In reality, Walt and his brother Roy, who was eight years older than Walt, did most of the work for their strict, domineering father. They woke up at 3:30 every morning to deliver newspapers to their 700 customers. Work was followed by school. For six years, Walt performed this dreary routine that left him no time for play.

ESCAPE INTO CARTOONING

Walt sought escape from the drudgery in art and entertainment. His teachers enjoyed his creativity and flair for performing. As a 10-year-old, Walt showed enough talent as an artist that his barber accepted drawings in exchange for haircuts.

In 1917, Elias Disney again grew restless and moved back to Chicago, where he obtained part ownership in a jelly factory. While attending McKinley High School in the city, Walt began to focus his attention on cartoons. He drew cartoons for the school newspaper, attended art classes at the Chicago Institute of Art, and went to every vaudeville show he could afford to get ideas for jokes and gags.

Walt managed to join the Red Cross ambulance corps as a driver in 1918, despite being only 16 years old. After spending 10 months in Europe at the end of World War I, he settled with Roy in Kansas City, hoping to make a career as an artist. Walt worked for a commercial art studio and a film advertising

company. In his spare time, he set up a crude studio in his garage, where he began experimenting with ways to turn his cartoons into animated films. Eventually, he interested enough local theaters in his films to risk starting his own company. Trying to make a living from his creative energy was difficult, however. After months of living in his office and eating beans out of a can to save money, Walt went bankrupt. In 1923, he decided to try his luck in a place where the entertainment industry was taking root: Hollywood, California.

After dabbling in acting as an extra in a cavalry film, Walt got the urge to give animation another try. With Roy serving as his business manager, he began putting films together. Single-minded in his

Walt Disney decorated the ambulance he drove for the Red Cross with a cartoon.

determination to succeed this time, he even used his dates with Lillian Bounds, whom he would marry in 1925, as occasions to scout out the movies of his competition.

SUCCESS WITH A MOUSE

Walt Disney met with distributors all over the country in an effort to get his films into theaters. Soon afterward, Disney dreamed up a new character—a cartoon mouse. "I . . . dressed my dream mouse in a pair of red velvet pants with two huge pearl buttons and composed the first scenario and was all set," he later recalled. After his wife objected to the name

Walt (second from left) and Roy Disney with their wives, Lillian (far left) and Edna (far right), and sister, Ruth, outside the Los Angeles Disney Bros. Studio

Mortimer, Disney changed the name of the character to Mickey.

Disney kept the drawing simple to allow for easier animation. He also became aware of new film techniques that allowed sound to be packaged into the film. As a smalltime operator with nothing to lose, Disney decided to experiment with these techniques. The result was a stunningly innovative use of music in the cartoon "Steamboat Willie." A national distributor took a chance on the film. Not expecting much, he signed only a one-year contract with Disney. When the film proved to be a box-office hit, Disney quickly found himself free of the restrictive contract terms that most small producers were locked into. He was able to negotiate a new deal with Columbia Pictures that let him retain ownership of his films and his studio's independence.

Mickey Mouse—with Disney providing the high-pitched voice—established the foundation for the Disney empire of short, animated films. Having trouble finding story lines for Mickey's likable but bland character, Disney surrounded him with more quirky characters, such as Donald Duck and Pluto.

Many different stories about the creation of Mickey Mouse exist. Some include several of Disney's partners in the invention; others say Disney was on a train by himself when he came up with the idea.

EXPANDING THE EMPIRE

Disney's films were popular, but he was concerned that each did little more than pay for the next one. Against Roy's advice, he took a chance on producing a full-length film in 1937, called *Snow White and the Seven Dwarfs*. The public loved it. Disney appeared to have finally made it big. His company grew from a handful of employees to more than 750 workers.

A scene from Snow White and the Seven Dwarfs, *Disney's first feature-length film. In 1939, Disney received an Academy Award for the film. He was presented with a very special Oscar—one full-size statue and seven miniature ones.*

This rapid growth nearly toppled Disney's fledgling empire. In the 1940s, World War II cut off his foreign markets, causing severe cash-flow problems. But Disney recovered after expanding into live-action nature documentaries and family films. He came up with a masterstroke of marketing by creating two television shows (*The Mickey Mouse Club* and *Disneyland*) that developed an eager market for his films. By the 1950s, Disney had become the biggest name in family entertainment.

Although he had entered the business in order to use his creativity, Disney gradually found more enjoyment in the business side of his career. Once, when Disney was asked about the most rewarding accomplishment of his life, he replied, "The fact that I was able to build an organization and hold it." This business interest led him to undertake a new challenge in the 1950s, one that was to have a significant impact on American culture.

DISNEYLAND PARK

In the early 1950s, Disney proposed to build an amusement park based on his characters. Many of his friends and associates questioned why such a successful entertainment giant would stoop to the role of a carnival operator. But Disney had something in mind completely different from the standard, low-budget amusement park. He intended to use the animation and robotic innovations his company had pioneered to bring his magical entertainment world off the screen and into an impeccably clean, orderly, real-life environment. It would be like allowing children to become part of a beloved Disney movie.

Disney took a great risk when he established Disneyland Park in Anaheim, California, in 1955. With bankers reluctant to back such a doubtful project and with little savings of his own, he borrowed on his life insurance to finance the plan's beginning stages.

Disneyland turned out to be such a success that it altered the very nature of amusement parks. Instead of being nearby places where the kids could spend an afternoon, amusement parks became family vacation destinations. As writer Max Apple observed, "Beginning with Disneyland, the amusement park moved from nickels and dimes into the realm of big business. . . ."

At Disneyland Park, Walt Disney and Mickey Mouse ride past Sleeping Beauty Castle in an old-fashioned fire engine.

AN EVEN BIGGER DREAM

Despite Disneyland Park's success, it did not meet Disney's high expectations. A man who was almost obsessed with controlling all situations he was in, he grew frustrated by the clutter of signs, motels, bars, fast-food restaurants, and cheap stores crowding in on his park, all trying to take advantage of the crowds flocking to Disneyland. For years, he complained that these places were spoiling the magical world he had tried to create. Disney dreamed of building another, better Disneyland somewhere in the eastern part of the United States. But this time he would make sure to own enough land to keep the fast-buck vultures far from its gates.

At the same time, he began to harbor even grander dreams. Instead of merely providing a temporary escape from the problems of the modern world, why not a permanent escape? Disney became convinced that private industry would have to take the lead in creating a better life for ordinary people. He proposed starting from scratch with a new city that would "influence the future of city living for generations to come"—a blueprint of the future and a place "where people actually live a life they can't find anywhere else today."

Few people thought Disney was serious when he first talked about his city of the future in 1958. But as he contemplated building a new Disneyland with a wide buffer zone to protect it from overcommercialization, he began to include his idea of a tightly controlled community run on state-of-the-art technology. Disney grew so excited over the possibilities that he began his days scribbling notes on napkins as he ate breakfast. He called together his most trusted advisors for secret brainstorming sessions at his Glendale, California, design headquarters. These people knew better than to dismiss any Disney idea, no matter how bizarre it sounded. Many of them had been on the receiving end of an impassioned scolding for not meeting his lofty expectations. "When I am excited, I get loud," Disney admitted. "Getting loud when I am excited is just my nature."

From 1958 to 1963, Harrison Price's Economics Research Associates performed four secret surveys in an effort to locate the best spot for what Disney's top executives called Project X. While putting together an exhibit for the New York World's Fair, Disney officials checked out a site near Niagara Falls. For a time, Disney's interest centered on St. Louis. But during a presentation to a group of St. Louis businesspeople, he mentioned that alcohol would not be allowed in his parks. This irritated August Busch, head of the largest brewery in the United States and one of St. Louis's most influential figures. The bad feelings that resulted soured Disney on St. Louis.

THE NEED FOR SECRECY

Eventually, Florida stood out as the most likely choice, mainly because its warm climate would allow an outdoor park to be open all year. Disney's researchers narrowed their choices down to three areas: Palm Beach, Ocala, and Orlando. The impending construction of a new interstate highway section near Orlando swung the balance in its favor. Over the next few years, Disney authorized nine more studies of the site, exploring such issues as state laws affecting the park, uses for land outside the park, and housing and lodging requirements. All of this needed to be done in secret, for two reasons.

First, the land presently was worth very little. Disney's wife reflected the opinion of real-estate experts when she commented during the early survey stages, "But it's just swamp, Walt! How could you possibly want anything here?" Such undesirable land could be purchased for very little. But the construction of a popular tourist attraction such as a new Disney amusement park would cause land values to skyrocket. If the landowners caught wind of his

Walt Disney points out the location chosen for his massive resort and amusement park in Florida. A diagram of the plan itself hangs behind Disney.

plans, they would jack their prices up so high that Disney might not be able to afford building on the huge scale that he had planned.

Second, there were many landowners with whom Disney would have to deal to buy the land. If motel and restaurant entrepreneurs knew he was building an amusement park near Orlando, they would rush in before Disney had completed all his land purchases and snatch up land as close to the facility as possible to take advantage of the crowds. Disney would find himself boxed in, just as he was at Disneyland Park in Anaheim.

In 1964, Disney assigned one of his lawyers, Robert Foster, the task of secretly buying the land he needed. Foster handled the job expertly. Although Florida newspaper reporters and others worked hard to crack the mystery of the secret land purchases, they were stumped. Within a year Foster was able to obtain 27,000 acres for the new project, compared to the 320 acres on which Disneyland in Anaheim rested. The average price per acre was only about $200, which meant that Disney had bought a piece of land twice the size of Manhattan Island for the bargain price of just over $5 million.

WALT DISNEY WORLD RESORT ARRIVES

Disney's concern over the effect that public knowledge about his project would have on land prices proved to be well founded. Almost immediately after the *Orlando Sentinel* finally uncovered the identity of the secret land purchaser in the fall of 1965, the real-estate market in central Florida went wild.

The Answer Uncovered

Walt Disney's Florida land scheme was uncovered in the autumn of 1965 by Emily Bavar, a reporter for the *Orlando Sentinel.* She happened to accept an invitation to attend the 10th anniversary of Disneyland. While there, she asked Disney if he had any plans to build another Disneyland Park in Florida.

"Who would ever want to build a theme park in Florida—with the sort of climate, rivers, and landscapes you have over there?" Disney scoffed. In giving his list of reasons why he would not build, however, Disney showed a remarkable knowledge of all the factors involved in building in Orlando.

Bavar began to suspect that Disney was trying to throw up a smokescreen. She asked him point-blank to confirm or deny that his agents were the mystery people buying up land near Orlando. When Disney avoided the question, Bavar sent a story back to the *Sentinel* in which she stated her case for believing that Disney was the mystery land purchaser. Florida's governor, Hayden Burns, confirmed the truth of her suspicions in a news conference a few days later.

The city of Orlando fueled the buying frenzy by putting a full-page ad in *Time* magazine touting itself as the future site of the new Disney park. According to one report, "It's estimated that more than 50 parcels, ranging from 10 acres to 5,000 acres, have changed hands—some at prices 12 times greater than before the Disney move was revealed."

Despite the enormous interest that Walt Disney World Resort generated, its construction created a number of bad headaches and anxious moments. According to Morgan Evans, the landscape supervisor for the park, "It was no-good land. It wasn't even good as pastureland. After massive earth moving, we probably had the world's worst soil in which

A portion of Disney's Orlando land, cleared in preparation for the construction of Walt Disney World Resort

to plant." Evans introduced half a million dollars' worth of exotic plants to the park before the place opened, all of which died—even after being given the utmost care. Disney's original plans for a technology-based community of around 20,000 permanent residents at Epcot ended up having to be scrapped because there was no legal way to enforce the many restrictions that Disney wanted to set for residents. Epcot was converted to a tourist/convention site.

The most disappointing element of the new park, however, was that, when it finally opened to the public in 1971, its creator was not around to enjoy the moment. Walt Disney died of circulatory system failure on December 15, 1966.

Future World

Walt Disney's Epcot (short for Experimental Prototype Community of Tomorrow) originally consisted of very elaborate plans. Disney considered Epcot the heart of his new project; he planned for the park to serve as a self-sufficient city that would focus on inventing and using new technology. The park was to be built in a radial design, with highways and mass transit moving outward from a central hub. People would live, work, and play in specific areas designated for each activity. Disney's plan included a layered system of transportation, with electric mass transit at the surface and automobiles and trucks on two underground levels. An industrial park located away from the middle of the city would contain computer centers and research and development labs.

How did Disney intend to make all this happen? He believed that American companies would give the technology they had developed to the Epcot community for free. Disney thought that once the city got started, businesses within Epcot would produce innovations for little or no profit. These innovations would then be distributed for the use of everyone in the Epcot community.

Disney planned to abolish property rights within the city as a way of keeping control over the businesses. Without any rights to their land, the businesses would not be able to make decisions about what to do with it. "There will be no landowners, and therefore no voting control," said Disney.

Disney's plans fell through. The Florida state government recognized that Disney's proposed policies would violate individual rights and refused to allow him to implement them.

Little of Disney's original plan now remains. Epcot became an elaborate amusement park. Divided into two sections, Future World and World Showcase, Epcot attracts millions of visitors every year. As a tribute to Walt Disney's love of technology, the Future World section of the park contains attractions and rides that focus on the development and history of technology, including communication and space technology. Some of the attractions in this section utilize ideas Disney came up with for his regulated community. World Showcase re-creates the culture of 11 different countries. Food and gifts are sold in buildings and along streets that replicate those in the countries they represent.

As an amusement park and educational center, Epcot has been an extremely profitable venture for the Walt Disney Company. New attractions are continually added, and old ones are refurbished. While more theme parks, along with restaurants and hotels, continue to spring up in the surrounding area, Walt Disney World Resort's Epcot and the Magic Kingdom Park have become some of the most popular tourist destinations in the United States.

LEGACY

As an entertainment pioneer, Walt Disney's influence is well documented. By introducing new animation techniques to the film industry and following them up with skillful and innovative marketing, he created a family entertainment empire second to none. By following through on his dream of a real-life Magic Kingdom in Disneyland Park and Walt Disney World Resort, he completely reshaped the concept of amusement parks—turning them from local, afternoon pastimes into family vacation destinations.

Disney's influence on the state of Florida has been just as remarkable. When Governor Hayden Burns introduced Walt Disney at a press conference on November 15, 1965, as the man "who will bring a new world of entertainment, pleasure, and economic development to the state of Florida," he was not exaggerating. By investing over $1 billion in Walt Disney World Resort, Disney planted an enormous tourist attraction in the empty flatlands of central Florida that generated many times that amount of income.

Perhaps the most dramatic measure of the effect Disney had as a real-estate investor lies in the city of Orlando. In 1965, Orlando's population stood at about 30,000. As soon as Disney announced his development plans in the area, Orlando blossomed into the fastest-growing city in the nation. Little more than a decade later, it was home to 250,000 people. By the mid-1990s, the city topped 1,600,000 and was still growing.

Walt Disney World's Magic Kingdom (above) is divided into sections with themes. Adventureland includes Pirates of the Caribbean, while Frontierland boasts the charms of Tom Sawyer Island. Tomorrowland houses Space Mountain, a roller coaster in the dark, and Fantasyland's rides involve characters such as Snow White and Peter Pan. Liberty Square re-creates colonial America in an array of old-fashioned shops and transportation. Epcot (right) is well known for its silver sphere, which houses a Future World attraction—Spaceship Earth—that illustrates the history of communication technology.

6

PAUL REICHMANN

OLYMPIA & YORK'S MASTER DEALER

In 1980, Richard Kahan was sweating bullets. He had been placed in charge of an urban renewal project that was an utter disaster. Battery Park City consisted of 93 acres of landfill—produced by the construction of the massive World Trade Center—on the tip of Manhattan Island. The city of New York had issued millions of dollars' worth of bonds to finance the development of this area but, after a dozen years of effort, had nothing to show for it. The World Trade Center was so huge that it had glutted the market for office space. One 44-story building on Sixth Avenue had been built at a cost of $100 million, only to stand empty for five years. At a time when other office buildings were having trouble finding tenants, developers saw no sense in taking

In his real-estate career, Paul Reichmann (b. 1930) took risks that other developers thought too dangerous or foolish and made his company successful despite the critics. He gambled on the stability of building in major cities around the world and made—and then lost—a fortune.

a chance on constructing another series of costly office buildings, especially in an unproven location. Now the bonds were coming due, and Kahan did not know where he would get the money to repay them.

The situation seemed hopeless—and then Paul Reichmann and his four brothers stepped in. They offered to take over the entire project and spend $189 million on buying the land, in order to develop six million square feet of office space within five years. Their proposal included a guarantee of $50 million to pay off the bondholders.

Kahan could hardly believe what he was hearing. He was ecstatic that the Reichmanns, alone among all those bidding for the land, understood his concern about the bonds. At the same time, he marveled at the brothers' boldness. This was an incredibly risky project in the current market, and yet the Reichmanns were willing to put all that cash on the line before they had a single tenant committed to moving in.

"These are the biggest crapshooters Manhattan has ever seen," Kahan declared.

Paul Reichmann was willing to take the risk because of three factors. He had faith that New York's position as a financial market would continue to raise the value of property in the city. Second, he recognized a trend toward larger floors so that different departments of companies could operate closely together instead of split up on several floors. Third, he had confidence that his company could handle the task without the delays and unexpected added costs common in the construction business.

crapshooter: slang for someone who takes high risks. The word comes from a gambling game called craps in which specific numbers rolled on two dice are needed to win.

Reichmann's judgment was correct. Five high-rise buildings were completed in 1988 on time and under budget. The Reichmann brothers were soon operating the World Financial Center, as the Battery Park City offices were named, at a profit.

Paul Reichmann's willingness to take incredible risks and his shrewd business judgment in determining which risks were worth taking created the largest real-estate development company in North America. At its peak, the Reichmanns' Olympia & York firm reached a value of $15 billion. But regardless of the brilliance of the gambler, no gambling streak lasts forever. When Reichmann's streak finally came to an end, he flamed out more spectacularly than any shooting star in the sky.

MIRACULOUS ESCAPE

The Reichmann family's story begins with Samuel Reichmann, an egg wholesaler in Beled, Hungary. Fearful of the Russians, who were threatening to attack Hungary in the 1920s, Samuel and his wife Renée fled across the border with their three children to Vienna, Austria, where Paul was born on September 27, 1930.

Forced to start a new career, Samuel bought a struggling glass factory and made it profitable. In 1938, the family was preparing for the bar mitzvah of their oldest son, Edward, when the boy's grandfather suffered a stroke. Hastily, the family moved the event to Beled so the grandfather could attend. While they were gone, Nazi mobs terrorized Vienna, assaulting Jews and vandalizing their property. The

The Reichmanns had a total of six children: a daughter and five sons. The eldest three—Eva, Edward, and Louis—were born in Beled, and the rest—Albert, Paul, and Ralph—were born in Vienna.

bar mitzvah: a religious ceremony in Judaism recognizing a 13-year-old boy as an adult in the eyes of the community

Paul Reichmann and his father, Samuel Reichmann, at the groundbreaking for the Toronto Star *building in 1969, 30 years after their escape from the Nazis*

Unlike many Orthodox Jews living in Vienna at the time, Samuel Reichmann paid close attention to the political and social climate in Austria. He read newspapers and listened to the radio intently. By the time the Gestapo went to the Reichmanns' home, Samuel had already been making plans to leave Austria.

German army swept into the country and began arresting Jewish businessmen. While in Beled, Samuel called home and learned that the Gestapo, the Nazi police, had come looking for him.

The Reichmanns never returned home; instead, they sought refuge in Paris. What the family viewed as a miraculous escape from the Nazis' murderous clutches would have a profound effect on the Reichmanns in future years. In thanks to God, they adhered strictly to Jewish laws and traditions even if they interfered with business. At the same time, they felt a sense of destiny that gave them the confidence to take risks that others shunned.

The safe haven of Paris proved to be short-lived. In June 1940, German forces shattered the French defenses and closed in on Paris from the north. The Reichmann family fled the city on foot on a road jammed with two million refugees. Eventually they drove 70 miles in a rented truck, then rode a train to the Spanish border. With what may have been black-market visas, they managed to work their way into pro-German Spain and make their way to the International Zone of Tangier in Morocco on the north coast of Africa. Here Samuel Reichmann again had to establish himself in a new business—this time as a currency trader and banker.

HUMANITARIAN

Originally, Paul had no interest in business. Influenced by his mother, his heart lay in social and humanitarian work. Renée Reichmann used the profits from her husband's business in order to send thousands of food parcels to inmates of Nazi concentration camps. "I remember the excitement of staying home from school certain days to help pack, or packing through the night and being able to sleep late," Paul recalled later in life.

In 1947, the 16-year-old left home for five years of religious instruction in Antwerp, Belgium, and Jerusalem, Israel, followed by college courses in London, England. When he returned to North Africa in 1953, Paul began working without pay as the education director of an organization that ran religious schools for poor Jewish immigrants living in Morocco. He supported himself during that time with a side job as a textile merchant.

The International Zone of Tangier was a specially chartered area established by a treaty signed by eight European nations. The zone was to be free of military occupation, and its economy became well known as a more relaxed market, especially for currency trading.

As the people he helped became able to restart their lives, Paul's relief organization was no longer needed. He decided to rejoin the family business. Meanwhile, Morocco moved toward independence on the rising current of the Islamic movement. As the international community of Tangier was absorbed into this Islamic state, the Reichmanns began looking, yet again, for a more favorable location.

NEW BUSINESS IN CANADA

Edward, the oldest Reichmann son, traveled to Canada to scout out the business possibilities there. He recommended that the family relocate to Toronto, and, in the late 1950s, the family took his advice. Once again, the Reichmanns were in a new land, scouting for a new business to run. With two partners and his brother Louis, Edward started a company in Montreal to import ceramic tiles from Spain. He named it the Olympia Trading Company.

The company grew so quickly that within a year it outgrew its rented warehouse. Dismayed by the $125,000 (Canadian dollars) price tag that contractors estimated for building a replacement, Louis and Edward figured they could save money by doing the work themselves. Sure enough, they built the warehouse for $70,000. This persuaded them to expand permanently into the construction business.

In the meantime, the three younger brothers, Albert, Paul, and Ralph, were more cautiously building their own tile import company in Toronto. They also followed the older brothers' lead by forming York Development to construct warehouses. They

Edward Reichmann's lawyer called to say that all the names Edward had wanted to use for his company were already taken. Edward happened to be unpacking his suitcase at the time, and he pulled out a pair of new socks with the brand name Olympia. Thus, the Olympia Trading Company was born.

Ralph Reichmann (b. 1934), Paul Reichmann's younger brother by four years

built warehouses that were better-looking and more sturdily constructed than those of their competitors for only two cents more per square foot. Before long, they were building more warehouses than all their competitors combined.

During the mid-1960s, Edward Reichmann's rapid expansion got his business into financial difficulties. The younger Reichmanns stepped in and bailed out their siblings by merging their businesses into what became known as Olympia & York. Surprisingly, it was Paul, the brother who had shown the least interest in business, who came to dominate the company.

The Olympia Trading Company's financial difficulties had a lot to do with Edward Reichmann. He tended to expand without taking the time to think about what he was doing. He didn't pay much attention to controlling costs and he often tied up his properties by using them as collateral on multiple loans.

INTO THE BIG TIME

In 1965, the Reichmanns stumbled into a deal that launched them into the world of large-scale development. All they wanted was a half-acre of land in order to construct a building with more stories than originally planned. The land they were looking at belonged to William Zeckendorf, one of the largest and most daring real-estate developers in North America. Legal issues prevented him from selling such a small amount of land. If the Reichmanns wanted the land, they would have to buy all of Zeckendorf's Toronto property—more than 500 acres. Included in this was a huge apartment development that Zeckendorf's company, Webb & Knapp, had begun and then had to abandon because of financial difficulties when it was half-complete.

William Zeckendorf (1904-1976) pulled off the biggest real-estate transaction in the history of New York City when he bought $53 million worth of Manhattan properties, including the Chrysler Building, in 1953. By 1965, however, his company's spectacular growth had left it short of cash and burdened with debt. In the same year that it sold its Toronto properties to the Reichmanns, Webb & Knapp declared bankruptcy.

At first glance it seemed ridiculous for the Reichmanns' tiny company to take on more than $17 million in debt to buy land they had not wanted just to get a half-acre. But Zeckendorf's demand forced them to consider the possibility, and they were surprised by what they found. Although they had no interest or expertise in managing residential property, they found the other properties attractive. According to Paul, "The more we analyzed the situation, the less risk there seemed to be. We couldn't figure out why the land hadn't been picked up, because it was in the geographical center of Toronto. Its value was much greater than what they were asking." Olympia & York made the deal.

Paul Reichmann skillfully resold the apartment complex, arranging a deal with the new buyers so that Olympia & York got its full investment back on the entire Zeckendorf properties and still controlled 400 acres of its own. The Reichmanns spent the next eight years developing this remaining property, and the huge profits they made provided the foundation for an even larger business deal.

FIRST CANADIAN PLACE

In 1973, Olympia & York fell into another unanticipated opportunity. The Reichmanns contracted to build new offices for the *Toronto Star* newspaper. When the *Star* moved into its new building, it left empty its old office building, located in the heart of Toronto's financial district. Paul Reichmann saw this as an opportunity for a bold masterstroke of development. The location was perfect for an office

The Toronto Star *building (left), built by Olympia & York*

building. If he could acquire the entire block on which the *Star*'s old offices were located, Olympia & York could demolish the buildings and construct an enormous skyscraper.

Reichmann was able to buy the *Star* building and all other structures on the block, except for the Royal Trust building. If he could not purchase that, he would have to abandon his whole plan. Recognizing his strong bargaining position, the owner of the building put it up for bid. When the sealed bids were opened, Olympia & York won only because it bid the exact figure it estimated for the value, $1,537,000, while its main rival rounded down to $1,500,000.

Many analysts thought the Reichmanns were crazy when they announced plans for a complex that included a 72-story building, the tallest in all of Canada. The analysts thought Toronto was already overbuilt with office space and that the Reichmanns would have trouble finding tenants. The critics were nearly right. First Canadian Place, as the complex was called, opened during a recession in 1982. It took Olympia & York four years—twice as long as anticipated—to lease it fully. But eventually First Canadian Place, with its vast office space and 165 shops and restaurants, became one of the most valuable and profitable properties in the city. At the same time, Olympia & York established itself as the world's most cost-efficient builder of skyscrapers.

First Canadian Place was not only the tallest building in Canada, but also the tallest building in the entire British Commonwealth (a loose collection of countries including the United Kingdom, Canada, and Australia, among others). In fact, First Canadian Place was the eighth tallest building in the world at the time.

ON TO NEW YORK

During construction of First Canadian Place, Paul Reichmann cast his eye on the biggest playing field in the real-estate business—New York City. In 1977, New York was teetering on the verge of bankruptcy. Most major investors were steering clear of the city, especially risky projects such as high-rise office buildings. But Paul Reichmann was willing to bet his company's future that New York would rebound. "Despite the bad news," recalled Albert Reichmann, "New York remained a diversified city, and we didn't believe it would lose its position as the world's leading financial center." The Reichmanns stunned the real-estate experts by investing about $334 million in eight rundown skyscrapers owned by the Uris Building Corporation.

Paul had guessed right. Almost as soon as the deal was completed, New York began to rebound. The extra care and attention the Reichmanns gave to their new buildings paid off in attracting new tenants. Many of the current tenants asked for more space. Within 10 years, office space that had sold for $30 per square foot when the Reichmanns bought it was worth $300 per square foot. The value of the Reichmanns' buildings soared by more than $2 billion.

Then the Reichmanns won a fierce bidding war to buy 237 Park Avenue, which had one million square feet of office space. They stripped the structure down to its frame, totally redesigned the offices, and installed a stunning 23-story atrium over a 7,000-square-foot courtyard. The Reichmanns followed up this success by taking on the risky Battery Park City project. They poured $1.5 billion into building the World Financial Center on a sandbar in the Hudson River. Architecture critics hailed the structure as a graceful addition to the skyline and a symbol of New York's revitalization.

The Toronto and New York deals vaulted the Reichmanns ahead of all the other development companies on the continent. By the late 1980s, the Reichmanns owned 40 office towers, controlled stock in a half-dozen major corporations, were among the biggest landlords in New York City, and had accumulated a net worth of $25 billion.

DEVOUT BILLIONAIRES

While amassing their empire, the Reichmanns never strayed from the principles that had guided them

Part of the Battery Park City Offices, more commonly known as the World Financial Center, in 1989

since their deliverance from the hands of the Nazis. The offices of Olympia & York closed early on Fridays to give all employees time to get home to observe the Jewish Sabbath (sundown Friday to sundown Saturday), and the Reichmanns included in all construction contracts a clause that specified that no work was to be done on the Jewish Sabbath. The Reichmanns preferred cooperation to intimidation in dealing with their employees, and, as a result, their employees never went on strike.

Despite their astounding wealth, the Reichmanns lived modestly. They had no corporate jets or limousines or fancy vacation homes. They lived within walking distance of the synagogue they attended,

Albert Reichmann (b. 1929), Paul Reichmann's older brother by one year, tried to avoid publicity.

"Paul knew perfectly well the risks he took and liked taking them. . . . He was a gambler."
—Robert Canning, financial confidant of Paul Reichmann

because they followed the Orthodox Jewish law of avoiding all physical work, including driving, on the Sabbath. Among the most charitable people in the business world, they gave away nearly $1 billion, much of it financing schools and synagogues.

None of the Reichmanns had any interest in publicity. In fact, they went to great lengths to avoid it. They never named buildings after themselves. They kept such a low profile that their own security guards occasionally failed to recognize them and refused to let them tour construction sites. Albert once hid behind a column for over an hour to avoid being photographed at a reception.

SEARCH FOR "IMPOSSIBLE" DEALS

Despite his devout lifestyle and shy, soft-spoken ways, Paul Reichmann was far from a pushover in business dealings. He researched possible investments and scoured the world's financial markets thoroughly. He could utterly exhaust people in negotiations. Most of all, he was a risk taker who thrived on the challenge of confounding the experts. "It became exciting to me to do different kinds of developments," he said. "There is an enjoyment in being able to do something that others consider difficult if not impossible."

Reichmann's desire to do the impossible led him to search for increasingly ambitious projects. In the late 1980s, he found one that dwarfed even his previous impressive deals. Having made a fortune betting on New York City's revival, Reichmann decided to place an even bigger bet on another great city. He became convinced that London was emerging as the financial capital of Europe and would soon be awash in demands for office space.

Encouraged by tax incentives from the British government, Reichmann put together a breathtaking proposal to construct 24 new office buildings, including a 60-story tower, in a seedy section of London along the Thames River. Noting that the area, known as Canary Wharf, was two miles from the city's financial district and was poorly served by transportation, his brothers opposed the plan. Their fears were reinforced by the lack of enthusiasm among British firms to relocate to Canary Wharf.

Paul, however, had no doubts about the project, which he claimed would make a lasting contribution to the economic well-being of London. "On a scale of 1 to 10—if the risk with [the World Financial Center] was 9—here it would be 1," he said. Olympia & York charged full-speed into construction. By 1990, it had spent $3 billion and had almost completed 12 of the buildings at Canary Wharf.

This time, however, Paul's legendary timing was off. In 1989, the London real-estate market had fallen into a prolonged depression. The Reichmanns were able to prelease just over half the available office space to foreign tenants and were unable to attract a single tenant from Great Britain.

Meanwhile, Olympia & York's other investments went into a tailspin. Its North American properties dropped in value. The billions of dollars that the Reichmanns had invested in oil stock evaporated as oil stocks took a plunge. But Paul tried to cover up

Paul Reichmann's Canary Wharf development, seen from across the Thames River

the problems, hoping that the market would rebound. Instead of selling other properties at a loss to finance the losses he was incurring, Paul borrowed against the property at Canary Wharf.

The financial situation, however, grew worse instead of better. In May 1992, Reichmann was so deep in debt that he had to surrender control of the Canary Wharf project to an administrator appointed by the court. Olympia & York declared bankruptcy. By the time the courts had finished dismantling the Olympia & York empire, the Reichmanns' $25 billion fortune had shriveled to a net worth of $100 million.

LEGACY

Paul Reichmann was the driving force behind one of the most powerful real-estate operations in history. His shrewdness and remarkable ability to control construction and financing costs led Olympia & York to undertake bold projects that changed the face of three of the world's greatest cities. Even Canary Wharf generated an operating profit after a new investment group put together by Paul Reichmann resumed construction at the site. "What Paul was excellent at was his ability to listen and ask questions of all sorts of people and then go off by himself and use his own brain finesse to improve on something," says one investment banker. "He was better than everybody at everything. For 25 years I said he was the most brilliant man I ever met."

Reichmann's days as the financial genius and giant of the real-estate development world, however, are over. If he had been more honest with his creditors and more careful about his choices of developments, he probably wouldn't have fallen so hard. Looking back on his career, Reichmann thought that his earlier stunning success may have "created character flaws that caused me to make mistakes." He had always taken higher and higher risks in his real-estate career. "Olympia & York most likely would have survived had Paul not been compelled continually to top himself as a developer," said one industry analyst.

7

THE GHERMEZIAN BROTHERS

THE MEGAMALL

In August 1992, a new shopping mall opened in Bloomington, Minnesota, that nearly took the breath away from first-time visitors. With a mind-boggling 330 stores surrounding an indoor amusement park, the Mall of America stretched the definition of a shopping mall far beyond anything seen before in the United States. Economic experts marveled at the audacity of the real-estate developers in risking hundreds of millions of dollars on such a grand scale. Millions of tourists flocked in from all over the nation and from foreign countries to see this wonder of the retail sales world.

There were four brothers, however, who were not at all impressed by the size and scale of the Mall

The Ghermezian brothers (left to right)—Raphael (b. 1944), Eskander (b. 1940), Nader (b. 1941), and Bahman (b. 1946)—developed the concept of the megamall, an enormous shopping and entertainment complex. They then built their vision into reality with the West Edmonton Mall and the Mall of America, the two largest shopping centers in the world.

of America. In fact, it was something of a disappointment to them. The project had been their idea, and their original plans called for a mall twice the size of the one that opened. The Mall of America was not even the largest mall that the brothers had built—their West Edmonton Mall in Canada was one million square feet larger. They had settled for the reduction only because they were unable to find the money to finance the construction their way.

No one could accuse the Ghermezian brothers of thinking small. They were the pioneers of a new concept in retail marketing—the megamall/entertainment complex.

CARPET MERCHANTS

The Ghermezians are an intensely private family who do not reveal much about their lives or early history. They trace their business roots back to 1895, when the family lived in Azerbaijan, a small republic located between the Black and Caspian Seas near the southeastern border of Russia. The Soviet Union absorbed Azerbaijan into its empire following the takeover by the Communists in 1917. In search of better economic opportunities and better living conditions, Jacob Ghermezian eventually moved his family to the Iranian capital of Tehran. There he developed a prosperous carpet export business. For reasons the Ghermezians choose not to explain, he and his family emigrated again in the late 1950s to Montreal, Canada—a striking parallel to the career path of a rival family of developers, the Reichmanns.

Jacob Ghermezian reestablished himself in the carpet import business in Montreal by selling Oriental rugs door to door. Before long, he opened a retail outlet for the rugs in Montreal. Gradually, his four sons, Eskander, Nader, Raphael, and Bahman, took over the operation of the Ghermezian Brothers stores. Business was so good that within five years, the Ghermezians expanded their operations into a chain of 16 stores, most of them in the United States.

INTO REAL ESTATE

Always on the lookout for a business opportunity, the brothers dabbled in real-estate purchases in the early 1960s. Although they bought land in Calgary, Alberta, and Vancouver, British Columbia, they focused most of their attention on the city of Edmonton, Alberta. Located far north of most population centers, on the edge of a windy prairie, land in Edmonton could be purchased for as little as $100 per acre. The Ghermezians counted on the city's growing production of oil to bring an increase in population that would make the land more valuable.

This proved to be the case. By the mid-1970s, the brothers had made so much money on their Edmonton property that they sold the carpet business and moved to the city in order to manage their investments there. For a while, their company, the Triple Five Corporation—a name whose origins are shrouded in mystery—mainly concentrated on dividing their suburban land holdings into lots that could be sold to home builders.

While doing so, they kept such a low profile that few people in Edmonton, much less the rest of Canada, had ever heard of them. The entire Ghermezian family, with wives and children, lived in two houses on a quiet street overlooking the North Saskatchewan River.

SECRECY AND CONTROVERSY

In May 1974, however, the brothers suddenly found themselves caught up in a political scandal. A former city alderman claimed that Raphael had offered him a $40,000 (Canadian) bribe to vote in favor of a zoning amendment favorable to the Ghermezians.

A lengthy government investigation ended with no charges filed. Although the Ghermezians refused all interview requests and even wrestled with photographers to keep from being photographed, their calm, publicity-free days were over. Their intensive lobbying of government officials for tax relief, zoning changes, low-interest loans, and tourism grants generated one wave of controversy after another. In the words of one analyst, "They have shown a remarkable ability to anger opposing local politicians while extracting tax concessions and rezoning approvals from the Edmonton city council."

It was the Ghermezians' insistence on secrecy that most rankled the politicians. Edmonton Mayor Laurence Decore was astounded to find that a Triple Five request for major government concessions on a huge development project had "less documentation supporting their proposal than would a group of Boy Scouts asking for a $1,000 grant."

The Ghermezians also had their supporters, who cited the brothers' active involvement with hundreds of schools, charities, and public interest groups as evidence of their trustworthiness. Allan Bleiken, a top official of a local government group promoting Edmonton's economic growth, explained, "They are unorthodox, so they are resented. They move at a faster, more intense pace than Canadians are used to—and that makes many of us uncomfortable."

The Ghermezians' unorthodox methods were indeed bewildering to supporters as well as opponents. Despite the mushrooming size of Triple Five, the brothers continued to run it like a small, private family business. Although each had his own area of expertise—Eskander handled the financial matters, Bahman managed the day-to-day operations of the business, Raphael oversaw the accounting, and Nader tended to lead the lobbying campaigns—all were included in every major decision the company made. People who had to negotiate with them had no idea who was in charge of what.

"Sometimes I felt like I was giving the same presentation four times," remarked one man who worked with them. "Different brothers come hurtling in and out of the room at all times, each wanting to know what was just said."

ATTRACTING MASSES TO THE COLD PRAIRIE

The Ghermezians did not let the bad publicity get in the way of their business plans. In 1976, Triple Five opened the Convention Inn South hotel and the Northwood Mall shopping center. In addition to their housing developments in the suburbs, they eventually constructed high-rise apartment buildings, hotels, and a nightclub in Edmonton.

But all of this was just a rehearsal for a grand scheme that the Ghermezians had first advanced during the 1967 Canadian Centennial celebration. Searching for a way to attract visitors to their shopping center properties in a cold, sparsely populated, out-of-the-way region, they proposed borrowing from Walt Disney's successful formula. Whereas Disney had taken the common amusement park and expanded it into a previously unimagined majestic world of entertainment, the brothers proposed to expand the ordinary shopping mall into a previously unheard-of royal extravaganza. The project that they brought before the Edmonton city council was so incredible that people could hardly believe they were serious. They wanted to turn 64 acres of suburban land on the west side into the largest shopping center in the world.

The plan faced a number of obstacles and criticisms before it could proceed. Once the scope of the project was revealed, those in the neighborhoods near the mall protested the coming increase in traffic. The Edmonton city council was hesitant to remove the many zoning restrictions that the project would violate. Other businesspeople in the city objected that such a huge mall would siphon all the customers away from their stores and cause them to go out of business. Both local and federal governments had to wrestle with Triple Five's requests for tax concessions. A deal was finally negotiated in which, in exchange for the many tax breaks, the Ghermezian brothers agreed to give all the profit from the mall's amusement park to local charity.

That was fine with the Ghermezians, because they planned to use the large indoor amusement park not as a source of profit, but as a lure. "We do not make money on the entertainment," Eskander explained. "We make money on the retail sales. But it is the entertainment that brings in the people."

THE "EIGHTH WONDER OF THE WORLD"

One by one, Triple Five was able to overcome all objections and opposition. Despite the fact that Alberta's slumping economy had discouraged most other developers from attempting major projects in the early 1980s, the Ghermezians proceeded with

Europa Boulevard, a shopping corridor reminiscent of a European street, inside the Ghermezians' Edmonton megamall

The Mindbender, one of the roller coasters inside the West Edmonton Mall

their bold proposal in three stages. The West Edmonton Mall opened in September 1981 with 220 stores, which made it a large, but not exceptional, mall. But the largest parking lot in the world, built to accommodate 20,000 vehicles, served notice that this was only the beginning.

In August 1983, the Ghermezians more than doubled the number of stores and installed the first of the mammoth entertainment facilities that they hoped would attract crowds from all over the world. In addition to the planned amusement park—which featured 47 rides, including giant roller coasters—they built a $5 million hockey arena into the complex.

In September 1985, the Ghermezians put the finishing touches on their revolutionary megamall.

They added another 386 stores and a water park with a 600-foot slide. Their crowning achievement was creating a 2.5-acre indoor lake, complete with a replica of Christopher Columbus's ship the *Santa Maria*, as well as a fleet of four yellow submarines capable of diving to 46 meters, which took visitors on a 30-minute tour of the undersea world.

In their efforts to promote their new creation, the Ghermezians let their imaginations run wild. They spent $750,000 (Canadian) at their grand opening on skydivers, pirates (to fight on the *Santa Maria*), and nearly half a million helium balloons. For overnight visitors, they constructed a 360-room Fantasyland Hotel with rooms decorated in fanciful themes.

In addition to housing a replica of the Santa Maria, *the West Edmonton Mall's Deep Sea Adventure includes a dolphin lagoon, where dolphins and their trainers give shows.*

The rooms in the Ghermezian brothers' Fantasyland Hotel were decorated around themes; some had beds shaped like carriages and pickup trucks, and one room had erupting volcanoes. This room, decorated with statues and fountains, evokes images of the Roman Empire.

The Ghermezians had succeeded in building what one developer called "the eighth wonder of the world." The West Edmonton Mall sprawled over 48 city blocks, and, with 5.2 million square feet of usable space, it was more than twice the size of the world's next largest mall. It boasted 836 stores, 110 restaurants, and 20 movie theaters, and employed 15,000 workers.

Impressive as it was, the mall was not built for show. "I don't work on glory," said Eskander Ghermezian. "[A project] has to make money before we will touch it." As it turned out, building the megamall was the easy part. Having gone deeply into debt to finance a project costing an estimated $500 to $700 million, the Ghermezians would have to attract millions of visitors a year to make it pay off.

With Edmonton's population at under 700,000, that meant bringing in a regular stream of visitors from around the world.

The Ghermezians hired a tourism director and spent more millions on advertising. The West Edmonton Mall quickly became Alberta's largest tourist attraction and drew more than 40 percent of its visitors from the United States. During the mid-1980s, the West Edmonton Mall was bringing in revenues of $280 per square foot, about twice the rate of an average mall. With the mall running profitably, Triple Five grew into one of Canada's largest companies, with assets of more than $4.3 billion. Employing a staff of 2,000 throughout the world, the Ghermezians expanded into other business areas, such as banking, where they formed People's Trust, Canada's second-largest nonpublic bank.

In 1985, Triple Five spent $85 million on advertising for the West Edmonton Mall alone.

SEARCH FOR THE ULTIMATE MALL

Believing that they had pioneered the mall of the future, the Ghermezians sought to build similar megamalls in other cities. They scouted locations in Burnaby, British Columbia, and Ontario, New York. They fleshed out a proposal to build a $1.8 billion, 9-million-square-foot shopping and entertainment complex in Oberhausen, Germany, that would have dwarfed the West Edmonton Mall, and an even more ambitious $5.8 billion shopping-office-leisure center project in Leeds, England. Every one of the projects, however, had to be abandoned either for lack of government cooperation or insufficient finances.

In 1985, however, the Ghermezians spotted a rare opportunity in the "Twin Cities" of Minneapolis and St. Paul, Minnesota. In 1982, Minnesota's professional baseball and football teams had moved from Metropolitan Stadium in Bloomington (a suburb of Minneapolis) to a domed stadium in downtown Minneapolis. With its stadium no longer operating, Bloomington was left with the unique situation of having 78 acres of land in a prime location available for development. The land was right along the major interstate highway beltline of the city, only a mile and a half from an international airport, and within easy distance of 7,000 hotel rooms. The city of Bloomington bought the land and then welcomed proposals from various developers.

Four vastly different proposals came before the Bloomington officials: 1) a series of office complexes, 2) residential condominiums, 3) a new Twin Cities convention/visitors center, and 4) a retail/entertainment mall. The last proposal came from the Ghermezian brothers, who saw this as their chance to top the West Edmonton Mall. Although Bloomington officials were staggered at first by the scale of the project that the Ghermezians proposed, they became convinced that it would work. Not only could the brothers point to the West Edmonton Mall as proof that such a megamall could be successful, but economic studies also showed that the Twin Cities had far fewer retail stores for its population than the national average.

In 1986, Bloomington officials signed a deal with the Ghermezians. It proved to be a savvy decision,

because each of the other options evaporated. The market for condominiums dropped dramatically, the Twin Cities experienced a glut in office space, and a downtown Minneapolis site was selected for the new convention center.

CHANGE OF PLANS

The Ghermezians were eager to get going on constructing a mall larger than the West Edmonton project, complete with indoor lakes and amusement parks. During 1986, they attempted to get approval for on-site work to begin within two months of when the architects began their drawings. However, they underestimated the time and effort involved in gaining all the required construction permits.

The building of the mega-mall was not the first time the Twin Cities had made history with a unique shopping development. In 1954, Edina (a suburb of Minneapolis) became home to the first enclosed, climate-controlled shopping center, Southdale Mall. Malls soon proliferated throughout the country, becoming standard features of the suburban landscape.

In the meantime, the Ghermezians' powerful business empire began to show cracks. After the initial curiosity wore off, the West Edmonton Mall became a heavy burden to its owners. According to one analyst, "The problem is that the mall is so big that it is hard to keep it fully leased." Some of the mall's tenants had difficulty paying their rent. An economic recession slowed down consumer spending. Although the mall still attracted crowds, the profits were barely enough to keep up with the enormous interest payments on the huge debt that the Ghermezians had incurred in building it. The brothers attempted to refinance the mall debt by selling bonds to investors, but they were unable to attract buyers. They missed property tax deadlines, which saddled them with more interest and penalties.

Because of these problems, it soon became apparent that Triple Five simply did not have the money to build the Mall of America, as the Bloomington Project became known. A business expert explained, "If you do not happen to have a lot of equity, you have to turn to a joint-venture partner." In other words, the cash-strapped Ghermezians needed to bring someone with money in as a partner, or the whole project would go down the tubes.

The brothers found two partners: Melvin Simon & Associates, one of the largest shopping-center developers and managers in the world; and Teachers Insurance and Annuity Association (TIAA), which brought the equity that the Ghermezians badly needed. TIAA would own 55 percent of the project and the Simons and Ghermezians 22.5 percent each.

Real-estate developers often look beyond traditional lenders, such as banks, to finance their projects. Insurance company and pension fund managers, for example, may invest their firms' assets in real-estate developments that they hope will appreciate in value over time. Teachers Insurance and Annuity Association (TIAA), a retirement fund for college professors, has $600 million invested in the Mall of America and is the property's largest owner. With more than $280 billion under management—including mortgages and real-estate investments worth more than $25 billion—TIAA is one of the most important investors in U.S. real estate today.

The Simons agreed with the Ghermezians' strategy of making a shopping mall "a destination rather than just a place to go buy a pair of pants and leave." They had recently converted some old downtown Indianapolis buildings into the Circle Center, an entertainment complex with stores, restaurants, movie theaters, and a virtual reality center. But the cost-conscious new developers scaled the Mall of America project back to about half its original size and finally broke ground for the building in June 1989. The Mall of America opened in August 1992, with 330 stores, 10,000 employees, and provision for 12,000 parking spaces.

Melvin Simon started his company in the 1960s to take advantage of Americans' changing shopping habits. He saw that suburban dwellers were willing to spend time driving to a clean place that offered a large variety of stores, so he and his brothers began building shopping malls. With 252 properties, Melvin Simon & Associates became the largest real-estate company in North America.

The Lego Imagination Center, or Legoland, a popular attraction at the Mall of America, offers an extensive display of large Lego people hard at work and a Lego building area, where parents and kids can rest and play.

LEGACY

By the time the Mall of America opened, the Ghermezians had declined from their position as one of the world's biggest and boldest large-scale developers. Due to financial difficulties that originated with the West Edmonton Mall and were compounded by other investment losses, the brothers sold off many of their properties and gave up control of major development projects in Edmonton in the late 1980s and early 1990s. In 1989, they abandoned Edmonton and moved to Toronto, where they hoped to reestablish their real-estate magic in the more conventional areas of apartment buildings and housing developments.

Regardless of their future success, they had already made their mark on society as the originators of the concept of the megamall. Both the West Edmonton Mall and the Mall of America had to overcome skeptics who found it hard to believe that such relatively small metropolitan areas could support retail complexes far larger than those in the world's largest cities. "[The Ghermezians] turn their dreams into reality," Edmonton's Mayor Decore had to admit. "They are incredible."

The Ghermezians' prediction that megamalls would be the wave of the future has yet to be proven. For the present, their megamalls stand as isolated wonders. While the West Edmonton Mall remains the world's largest in size, the Mall of America has surpassed it as a tourist magnet. The complex quickly filled all of its 4.2 million square feet of rental space.

A corridor inside the Mall of America

With 520 specialty stores, 83 restaurant and food outlets, 8 nightclubs, 14 movie screens, and a 7-acre indoor Camp Snoopy amusement park as enticements, the Mall of America has consistently drawn between 35 and 42 million visitors a year. That total is more than the combined annual total of visits to the Grand Canyon, Disneyland, and Graceland. More than 40 percent of these were out-of-state visitors, who brought more than $1 billion in tourist revenues to the state of Minnesota.

Although the Ghermezian brothers handed control of the Mall of America project to Melvin Simon & Associates very early in the developmental stages, Bloomington Mayor Kurt Laughinghouse says that it never would have happened without them. "The credit goes to the Ghermezians," he says, "for promoting the idea and making it believable."

The Mall of America's amusement park, Knott's Camp Snoopy, includes a ferris wheel and the Pepsi Ripsaw roller coaster in its list of rides.

Melvin Simon & Associates and Triple Five hope to eventually enlarge the Mall of America to more than 9 million square feet. This second phase of construction would make the mall the largest single retail complex in the world.

GLOSSARY

appreciate: to rise in value, especially over time

auditor: an examiner of records or financial accounts who checks for accuracy

bankrupt: having been legally determined as unable to pay back one's debts. A court then divides up the debtor's property among the creditors.

bar mitzvah: a Jewish ceremony recognizing a 13-year-old boy as an adult in the eyes of the community

collateral: property offered against a loan in case the debtor cannot pay it back

comptroller-general: an official designated to supervise finances for a government or corporation

contract: a legally binding, written agreement between two or more people

contractor: someone who agrees to provide services and/or material, usually for construction work, for a certain price

crapshooter: slang for someone who takes high risks. The word comes from a gambling game called craps in which specific numbers rolled on two dice are needed to win.

creditor: a person or company that has loaned money not yet paid back

debtor: a person or company who owes money to someone else

depression: a period of drastic decline in business production and of high unemployment

down payment: money paid immediately for a purchase, with the remainder to be paid later

embargo: specifically, a government ban on shipping, but also used for any kind of ban

finances: money, usually of a government or corporation

foreclose: to assume ownership of land that has been mortgaged, usually when payments have not been made; *see also* **mortgage**

impeachment: the charging of a public official with improper conduct in office

invest: to commit money to some enterprise, usually a business, in order to get more money or some other value in return

lease: the contract between a tenant and a building owner that outlines the terms and conditions of the tenant's stay in the building; *see also* **tenant**

military installation: a permanent military base

mogul: a person who is very rich or powerful

mortgage: a temporary pledge of property to a creditor until a loan is paid back

pay claim: a form submitted to a government or company that requests money owed for services or labor already performed

real estate: land and whatever is on it, including any natural resources and developments

recession: a period of general decline in business activity

rent revenues: money brought in to an owner of properties from rent paid by tenants

shareholder: someone who owns a portion of a company, in the form of shares of stock

speculation: investment in land or any other commodity in the hope of a quick, large profit

surveying documents: papers outlining the results of surveying, or the measuring of the distances and the elevations of a piece of land

tenant: someone who rents property, such as office space or an apartment, from the owner of a building

tycoon: a rich businessperson or industrialist

BIBLIOGRAPHY

Alexander, Tom. "What Del Webb is Up to in Nevada." *Fortune*, May 1965.

Apple, Max. "Uncle Walt." In *Fifty Who Made the Difference*, edited by Lee Eisenberg. New York: Villard Books, 1984.

Arbuckle, Robert D. *Pennsylvania Speculator and Patriot: The Entrepreneurial John Nicholson, 1757-1800*. University Park, Pa.: Penn State University, 1975.

Arnebeck, Bob. "Tracking the Speculators: Greenleaf and Nicholson in the Federal City." *Washington History*, Spring/Summer 1991.

Bianco, Anthony. *The Reichmanns: Family, Faith, Fortune, and the Empire of Olympia & York*. New York: Random House, 1997.

———. "Faith and Fortune." *Business Week*, January 20, 1997.

Bliven, Bruce, Jr. *New York: A History*. New York: Norton, 1981.

Burns, Ric, and James Sanders. *An Illustrated History of New York*. New York: Knopf, 1999.

Burrows, Edwin G., and Mike Wallace. *Gotham: A History of New York to 1898*. New York: Oxford University Press, 1999.

Daly, John. "Blue-sky Planning." *MacLeans*, August 21, 1989.

———. "Cloning a Giant Mall." *MacLeans*, December 22, 1986.

"Disney's Wider World." *Business Week*, December 25, 1965.

Finnerty, Margaret. *Del Webb: A Man, A Company*. Flagstaff, Ariz.: Heritage, 1991.

Foster, Peter. *Towers of Debt: The Rise and Fall of the Reichmanns*. Toronto: Key Porter Books, 1986.

Hazel, Debra. "World's Largest Mall At a Crossroads." http://www.icsc.org/srch/sct/current/sct0400/01.html, cited May 23, 2001.

Henry, Gordon M. "Welcome to the Pleasure Dome." *Time*, October 27, 1986.

McCabe, James D., Jr. *Great Fortunes and How They Were Made*. Freeport, N.Y.: Books for Librarians, 1870.

McMurdy, Deirdre. "Glitter Without Gold." *MacLeans*, July 29, 1991.

Mall of America. "History of the Mall." http://www.mallofamerica.com, cited May 16, 2001.

"Man on the Cover." *Time*, August 3, 1962.

Minnigerode, Meade. *Certain Rich Men*. Freeport, N.Y.: Books for Librarians, 1927.

Mosley, Leonard. *Disney's World*. New York: Stein and Day, 1985.

"A Place in the Sun." *Time*, August 3, 1962.

Powell, Jim. *Risk, Ruin and Riches: Inside the World of Big-Time Real Estate*. New York: Macmillan, 1986.

Riha, John. "Mall Moguls." *Northwest Airlines World Traveler*, March 1998.

Rosenbaum, Ron. "The House That Levitt Built." In *Fifty Who Made the Difference*, edited by Lee Eisenberg. New York: Villard Books, 1984.

Salter, Michael. "The Ghermezians' Secrets." *MacLeans*, April 15, 1985.

Schickel, Richard. "Bringing Forth the Mouse." *American Heritage*, April 1968.

Smith, Arthur D. Howden. *John Jacob Astor: Landlord of New York*. Philadelphia: Lippincott, 1929.

Southdale Mall. "Origins of Southdale." http://www.southdale.com, cited May 16, 2001.

"Spreading Webb." *Time*, January 26, 1962.

Trillin, Calvin. "A Reporter At Large." *New Yorker*, April 4, 1964.

Trump, Donald, with Tony Schwartz. *Trump: The Art of the Deal*. New York: Random House, 1987.

"Up From the Potato Fields." *Time*, July 3, 1950.

Watts, Steven. *The Magic Kingdom: Walt Disney and the American Way of Life*. Boston: Houghton-Mifflin, 1997.

"Where the Buck Stops." *Forbes*, September 1, 1968.

Zehren, Charlie. "The Dream Builder." http://www.lihistory.com/specsec/hslevpro.htm, cited May 16, 2001.

SOURCE NOTES

Quoted passages are noted by page and order of citation.

Introduction

p. 15 (first): Anthony Bianco, *The Reichmanns: Family, Faith, Fortune, and The Empire of Olympia & York* (New York: Random House, 1997), 370.

p. 15 (second): Anthony Bianco, "Faith and Fortune," *Business Week* (January 20, 1997), 62.

p. 16 (caption): Donald Trump with Tony Schwartz, *Trump: The Art of the Deal* (New York: Random House, 1987), 3.

pp. 16-17: Trump, *The Art of the Deal*, 3.

Chapter One

p. 19: Robert D. Arbuckle, *Pennsylvania Speculator and Patriot: The Entrepreneurial John Nicholson, 1757-1800* (University Park, Pa.: Penn State University, 1975), 18.

p. 24: Arbuckle, *Pennsylvania Speculator*, 2.

p. 31: Arbuckle, *Pennsylvania Speculator*, 115.

p. 32: Arbuckle, *Pennsylvania Speculator*, 124.

p. 35: Arbuckle, *Pennsylvania Speculator*, 138.

Chapter Two

p. 37: James D. McCabe Jr., *Great Fortunes and How They Were Made* (Freeport, N.Y.: Books for Librarians, 1870), 78.

p. 39 (first): McCabe, *Great Fortunes*, 62.

p. 39 (second): McCabe, *Great Fortunes*, 63.

p. 42: Edwin G. Burrows and Mike Wallace, *Gotham: A History of New York to 1898* (New York: Oxford University Press, 1999), 411.

p. 44: Meade Minnigerode, *Certain Rich Men* (Freeport, N.Y.: Books for Librarians, 1927), 42.

p. 45: Minnigerode, *Certain Rich Men*, 43.

p. 47 (margin): McCabe, *Great Fortunes*, 68.

p. 47 (first): Ric Burns and James Sanders, *An Illustrated History of New York* (New York: Knopf, 1999), 51.

p. 47 (second): Burrows and Wallace, *Gotham*, 337.

p. 50: Burns and Sanders, *Illustrated History*, 51.

p. 51 (margin): McCabe, *Great Fortunes*, 90.

p. 51: McCabe, *Great Fortunes*, 88.

p. 52: Burns and Sanders, *Illustrated History*, 51.

p. 53: Minnigerode, *Certain Rich Men*, 49.

Chapter Three

p. 56: Ron Rosenbaum, "The House That Levitt Built," *Fifty Who Made the Difference* (New York: Villard Books, 1984), 307.

p. 59: Rosenbaum, "The House That Levitt Built," 310.

p. 61 (margin): Rosenbaum, "The House That Levitt Built," 310.

p. 62: "Up From the Potato Fields," *Time* (July 3, 1950), 70.

p. 64: Rosenbaum, "The House That Levitt Built," 306.

p. 66: "Potato Fields," 72.

p. 68 (margin): Rosenbaum, "The House That Levitt Built," 305.

p. 68 (first): Rosenbaum, "The House That Levitt Built," 312.

p. 68 (second): Rosenbaum, "The House That Levitt Built," 304.

p. 69 (first): "Potato Fields," 69.

p. 69 (second): Rosenbaum, "The House That Levitt Built," 320.

p. 70 (margin): "Potato Fields," 67.

Chapter Four

p. 75 (margin, first, and second): "Man on the Cover," *Time* (August 3, 1962), 49.

p. 77: "Where the Buck Stops," *Forbes* (September 1, 1968), 49.

p. 81 (first): Calvin Trillin, "A Reporter At Large," *New Yorker* (April 4, 1964), 172.

p. 81 (second): Trillin, "A Reporter At Large," 172.

p. 82 (margin): Margaret Finnerty, *Del Webb: A Man, A Company* (Flagstaff, Ariz.: Heritage, 1991), 95.

p. 83: "A Place in the Sun," *Time*, August 3, 1962, 47.

p. 84 (margin): Trillin, "A Reporter at Large," 120.

p. 88: Trillin, "A Reporter At Large," 120.

p. 89: "Man on the Cover," 49.

Chapter Five

p. 96: Richard Schickel, "Bringing Forth the Mouse," *American Heritage* (April 1968), 24.

p. 99 (first): Schickel, "Bringing Forth the Mouse," 94.

p. 99 (second): Max Apple, "Uncle Walt," *Fifty Who Made the Difference* (New York: Villard Books, 1984), 113.

p. 101 (first): Steven Watts, *The Magic Kingdom: Walt Disney and the American Way of Life* (Boston: Houghton-Mifflin, 1997), 424.

p. 101 (second): Jim Powell, *Risk, Ruin and Riches: Inside the World of Big-Time Real Estate* (New York: Macmillan, 1986), 345.

p. 101 (third): Apple, "Uncle Walt," 119.

p. 102: Leonard Mosley, *Disney's World*, (New York: Stein and Day, 1985), 281.

p. 104: Mosley, *Disney's World*, 281.

p. 105: "Disney's Wider World," *Business Week* (December 25, 1965), 21.

pp. 105-106: Mosley, *Disney's World*, 283.

p. 107: Watts, *The Magic Kingdom*, 444.

p. 108: Watts, *The Magic Kingdom*, 421.

Chapter Six

p. 112: Powell, *Risk, Ruin and Riches*, 43.

p. 115: Bianco, "Faith and Fortune," 58.

p. 119: Powell, *Risk, Ruin and Riches*, 34.

p. 121: Powell, *Risk, Ruin and Riches*, 37.

p. 124 (margin): Bianco, *The Reichmanns*, 370.

p. 124: Bianco, "Faith and Fortune," 62.

p. 125: Bianco, "Faith and Fortune," 68.

p. 127 (first): Bianco, "Faith and Fortune," 64.

p. 127 (second): Bianco, "Faith and Fortune," 69.

p. 127 (third): Bianco, "Faith and Fortune," 56.

Chapter Seven

p. 132 (first): Michael Salter, "The Ghermezians' Secrets," *MacLeans* (April 15, 1985), 34.

p. 132 (second): Salter, "The Ghermezians' Secrets," 35.

p. 133 (both): Salter, "The Ghermezians' Secrets," 35.

p. 135: Gordon M. Henry, "Welcome to the Pleasure Dome," *Time* (October 27, 1986), 75.

p. 138 (first): Deirdre McMurdy, "Glitter Without Gold," *MacLeans* (July 29, 1991), 38.

p. 138 (second): Henry, "Welcome to the Pleasure Dome," 75.

p. 142 (first): McMurdy, "Glitter Without Gold," 38.

p. 142 (second): John Daly, "Cloning a Giant Mall," *McLeans* (December 22, 1986), 30.

p. 143: John Riha, "Mall Moguls," *Northwest Airlines World Traveler* (March 1998), 52.

p. 144: Salter, "The Ghermezians' Secrets," 35.

p. 145: Daly, "Cloning a Giant Mall," 30.

INDEX

Walt Disney World Resort, 101-104, 105-106, 107, 108, 109. *See also* Disneyland Park; Magic Kingdom Park

War of 1812, 44

Washington, D.C., 19, 20, 30-33, 34-35

Washington, George, 13-14, 30, 31

Webb, Del: as baseball player, 73, 74, 75; casinos invested in, 78, 87; in construction business, 73, 74, 76-79; death of, 87-88; early real-estate investments of, 79-80; early years of, 74-75; New York Yankees owned by, 78, 87; personality of, 76, 77, 87; Sun City created by, 2, 73, 74, 80-86, 87, 88-89; wealth of, 78, 79, 87-88

Webb, Hazel Church (first wife), 75

Webb, Jimmy (grandfather), 83

Webb & Knapp, 118

West Edmonton Mall, 129, 130, 135-139, 140, 141, 142, 144

Wilson, James, 26-27

World Financial Center, 113, 122, 123, 125. *See also* Battery Park City

World Trade Center, 111

World War I, 75, 94

World War II, 55, 58, 60, 76, 77, 98

York Development, 116, 117

Youngtown, 80

Zeckendorf, William, 118, 119

ABOUT THE AUTHOR

Nathan Aaseng is an award-winning author of more than 100 fiction and nonfiction books for young readers. He writes on subjects ranging from science and technology to business, government, politics, and law. Aaseng's books for The Oliver Press include five titles in the **Business Builders** series and nine titles in the **Great Decisions** series. He lives with his wife, Linda, and their four children in Eau Claire, Wisconsin.

PHOTO CREDITS

Archive Photos: front cover (center), pp. 34, 43, 44

The Art Institute of Chicago: pp. 18, 22

Del Webb Corporation: pp. 2, 72, 74, 75, 76, 78, 81, 82, 83, 84, 85, 86, 88, 89

Dictionary of American Portraits (published by Dover Publications, Inc., 1967): p. 53

©Disney Enterprises, Inc.: pp. 90, 93, 95, 96, 98, 100, 103, 105, 106, 109 (both)

Levittown Historical Society: p. 60

Levittown Public Library: front cover (top left), pp. 54, 56, 57, 63, 64, 65 (bottom), 67

Library of Congress: front cover (bottom right), pp. 11, 12, 14, 21, 26, 30, 31, 32, 33, 35, 36, 46, 71

Mall of America: pp. 143, 144, 145

National Archives: pp. 65 (top), 141

New York Historical Society: pp. 45, 48, 49

New York Public Library: pp. 6, 38, 51, 52

Timepix: pp. 118 (John Loengard), 123 (James Keyser)

Toronto Star: pp. 110 (T. Bock), 114 (F. Lennon), 117, 120 (G. Bezant), 124, 126 (K. Argue), 128 (D. Cooper)

The Trump Organization: pp. 16, 17

West Edmonton Mall: pp. 135, 136, 137, 138, back cover